Contents

Carbolics

Carbolics

A Personal Motoring Disinfectant

JAMES MAY

HODDER &
STOUGHTON

First published in Great Britain in 2022 by Hodder & Stoughton
An Hachette UK company

1

Copyright © James May 2022

A CIP catalogue record for this title is available from the British Library

Hardback ISBN 9781399713702
eBook ISBN 9781399713719

Typeset in Plantin Light by Hewer Text UK Ltd, Edinburgh
Printed and bound in Great Britain by Clays Ltd, Elcograf S.p.A.

Hodder & Stoughton policy is to use papers that are natural, renewable
and recyclable products and made from wood grown in sustainable
forests. The logging and manufacturing processes are expected to
conform to the environmental regulations of the country of origin.

Hodder & Stoughton Ltd
Carmelite House
50 Victoria Embankment
London EC4Y 0DZ

www.hodder.co.uk

Contents

Carbolics

Introduction

DriveTribe was a brilliant idea. A digital platform, free to use and open to everyone, that would democratise the rather exclusive profession that had provided me with a living for thirty years, and in doing so spawn a new and more numerous generation of writers, photographers and film-makers to populate the bollocksphere of motoring journalism.

I was one of the founders and investors in the business, and it amused me to think that I would eventually reap a handsome dividend through, in effect, the process of making myself redundant. A lot of people who have been fortunate in their fields talk of 'giving something back' and so did I, although in private I was thinking more in terms of a nice motorboat.

It went bust.

This annoyed me. Yes, I'd put a lot of money into DriveTribe and it was all gone, but I'm not bitter about that (even though I mention it here). Business is naught but a bagatelle. What really annoyed me was that the great canon of writing I had contributed to the enterprise just disappeared.

When a book goes out of print it will probably be completely forgotten (they tend to go out of print for a reason). But one or two will survive in libraries or lofts and might be rediscovered and reappraised, like Shelley's *Poetical Essay on the Existing State of Things* (1811). The same might be true of a 1928 Lagonda with coachwork by Scrotum & Wingback found in a barn (see p. 29).

But when an app and its associated website are taken down, the content simply vanishes as a binary fart and isn't going to be rediscovered between the pages of an old encyclopaedia. These essays were once available globally after a few clicks; suddenly, they existed only on the hard discs in my drawer of abandoned laptops.

So here they are again, in the only form known to me when I started in journalism, in print. This book can be read and then left on a shelf for your descendants to discover during the inevitable house clearance, and then thrown in the bin.

Let's talk about secs

I don't know who the first people were to quote a 0–60mph or 0–100kmh time for a car, but it must have been a long time ago. These figures have been around for as long as I've been reading about cars, and that's almost half the lifetime of the car as a credible idea. Anyway, I wish they hadn't.

As beardy archaeologists say when they unearth half a Viking pot or whatever, 'What does it mean?' Not as much as you might think, actually, and without wishing to get too bogged down in amateur physics, here's why.

Acceleration, as a real physicist will tell you if you're unlucky enough to be cornered by one, is defined as 'the rate of change of velocity'. What this means in normal English is how quickly something goes more quickly.

Let's take the example of the most universally understood and experienced accelerative force on the planet, which is gravity. In round figures, gravity will accelerate a falling thing at the rate of 10 metres per second per second; that is, if you come over all Galileo and drop a metal ball from a tall building, it will be going 10 metres per second faster for every second that passes. (This sort of thing, by the way, ignores all the annoying stuff that stops physics working properly, such as air resistance. Also known as reality. But let's not worry about it.)

Here's the first problem with 0–60mph times: '4.8 seconds' or '8.6 seconds' are not measures of acceleration, they are simply measures of time. I know this sounds a bit pedantic, but to express acceleration properly we need speed *and* time, to show how quickly the speed is increasing. Rate of change of velocity, see?

The second problem is that cars don't accelerate like a Renaissance boffin falling off a wonky tower in Pisa.

Gravity makes things accelerate at a constant rate. Cars rarely do that.

Take two examples from my own motoring history. My current electric BMW i3 does 0–60mph in 7.2 seconds. The Ford Fiesta RS1800 I owned way back in the 1990s did it in 8.3 seconds. So the BMW is faster. But it doesn't accelerate as fast as the Fiesta did. Wait for it . . .

The BMW, being electric, has a very flat torque curve and accelerates in a very linear way. The crudely turbocharged Fiesta went off the line in the rather sluggish manner of any other hatchback, but when the turbo finally kicked in at about 4000rpm the view through the screen went all squiffy like it did on the *Starship Enterprise* at warp speed, and my eyeballs changed shape. Only briefly, mind.

The point is this. As car enthusiasts interested in cheap thrills, the rate of acceleration is what excites us. It's what presses us into the seat and makes us snigger. The BMW arrives at 60mph before the Fiesta, but 60mph is merely a speed. The peak metres per second per second figure in the Ford was higher.

And that's what car makers should be quoting.

Doing it with the fox on

Doing it with me fez on

I would never go to the supermarket naked, and that's exactly why I can't own a Ferrari 488 Spider.

I like the 488 Spider – it's the GTS, if you're into the accepted nomenclature stuff. There have been criticisms about the turbocharged engine, because the high-rev Italian histrionics of the old naturally aspirated version have been lost, but that honestly doesn't bother me that much. I have a bike with an engine that'll rev to 15,000rpm if I want to marvel at the thought of valves moving that quickly.

The door handles look completely crap. No idea what they were thinking of there. More worryingly, it's a bit creaky on anything other than a perfect road, and I hate cars that sound like the *Cutty Sark*. It's the convertible, you see, and that leads me to a very important question.

Whenever I drive a convertible, and I reach for the button or lever that lowers the top, I pause and think, *Would I take the roof down if I was naked?* I did take roofs down when I was in my thirties, and my protruding head was a wild cataract of hairy glory and my face was stretched over my skull like the baize on a newly assembled pool table. But I'm fifty-three now, and I look like shit.

In fact, if I'm in a Ferrari at all, let alone a convertible one, I look like a middle-aged man who's worried that women don't find him interesting any more. That's why I have one.

But back to nudity. If you're my sort of age, you shouldn't have a convertible car at all. But if you do, and you're thinking of lowering the roof, stop and ask yourself this question. Would I be happy now if people could see my old chap/magic triangle?

If not, leave it up.

A small cheeseburger

I absolutely bloody love mid-engined supercars. They make me deeply happy, and I honestly believe that any nagging first world problem I may be suffering can be dispelled by having an engine behind my head and a stubby bonnet in front of my face. How's that for a first world solution?

Obviously, supercars are completely pointless and fail epically at the job of being a useful car. A supercar confers no special attribute on its owner or driver, and I've pointed out many times that no one ever ran down the aisle of an airliner in a massive panic shouting, 'Is there anyone on board who can drive a supercar?'

In which case, I'm free to consider the supercar as

an artwork (Ovid stated that one of the definitions of true art is that it has no utility) or maybe just a pleasant experience, like one of those Indian head massages or a light jazz cigarette. It's important that they can do all that Nürburgring stuff because that gives them meaning, but they slot into my life as simply 'nice'.

The McLaren 540C is very nice. This is the 'budget' McLaren (where the meaning of 'budget' depends on whether you scavenge for a living on a rubbish tip or you're Jeff Bezos) and does away with some of the complex hydraulic suspension stuff of the grander versions and uses steel anti-roll bars instead. At around £130,000, it's in the same drop zone (sorry) as Honda's NSX, but whereas the Honda is a very clever multi-motor hybrid, the McLaren is essentially old-school.

Actually, that's not entirely fair. Just as the Honda has brought the technology of the Porsche 918, the LaFerrari and indeed McLaren's P1 to the realm of the common supercar, McLaren has, with the 540C, popularised the exotic of ten or so years ago: carbon-fibre tub, twin-turbo engine, adaptive and configurable suspension, and so on. All stuff that was as unattainable as the moon not so long back. So I'll take none of your 'entry level' snootiness in this tribe. This is a 533bhp supercar that'll do 199, mister. I never once found it a bit underpowered and I haven't yet been round a bend and thought, *Oh no! The suspension's all full of steel bits!*

There are, however, a few banal things to be criticised. I find the steering a bit light and the engine note very ordinary, even with the sports exhaust fitted here. The gearshift is perfectly fine, but not as crisp as the PDK job on a Porsche. My car had the optional carbon-ceramic brakes fitted, at an extra £7,290, but I'd throw those in the canal and ask for the standard clog-iron bits to be put back on, because carbon-ceramic makes a funny noise, and admitting you have opted for such a thing makes you a bit of a knob and a helmsman. I'm not interested in being a helmsman; I'm here for the art.

On the plus side, the ride has a lovely sophisticated firmness to it and the view out of the screen is fab. It's a creak-free car (unlike some rivals I've driven recently) and a lot of the detailing is really tasteful: the column stalks, for example, and the instrument display.

Anyway, back to thinking about it in terms of

niceness. This definitely isn't an Italian supercar, because it isn't theatrical enough. Next to a 488 or Huracan it could be described, as my mother would say, as 'very plain', although at least the doors open in an exciting way. It definitely isn't German, either, as it doesn't make enough sense and it's too mid-engined. It's quite techy and purposeful, and the fascia glows in a fascinating and enticing manner, but it doesn't have much in the way of cultural baggage. Maybe it's sort of Swiss.

Or maybe – here's a thought – it's a proper piece of modern Britain, and what a relief that is. There are no heritage hang-ups to confuse the design, and no bling in the cabin. No suggestion of aprons, fake history or faux artisanship lurking in the background. It's built in a modern factory in an unassuming place and feels like the work of people who are entirely focused on automotive engineering and how it can be made to interact with your bits.

And yet . . . it's still homespun enough to feel like a cottage-industry car, where the cottage is more like a hospital and you're expected to wipe your feet and not make too much noise. The graphics on the central screen are a bit last generation, there are a few mechanical clunks and whirs making their way through, and even the click in the paddle shift has a slight 'early Amstrad' feel to it. It's built, rather than entirely manufactured, which makes it feel nice and personal. (It is, of course. If you order one, you can go along and watch it being built, so long as you wash your hands and don't touch anything.)

I've said before that some cars seem to be smiling as you drive along in them, and the 540C is one such. It's a good-natured supercar, loved by casual onlookers and positively adored by my missus, who (if she's honest) hates my Ferrari. The hackneyed view of McLaren is that everybody there has OCD and as a result they produce a functional but sterile car. Total bollocks. A machine is like a book, as someone once said, if you know how to read it. The 540C feels very, very special to me, a perfect blend of elemental supercar sensations with iPad-era contemporary trimmings. I'm delighted Britain can produce such a thing – not because I'm hamstrung about being British, but because I think it's important.

You're right, this isn't the fastest supercar in the

world. In fact, it's the slowest supercar in Woking. But note that I haven't bothered you too much here with stuff about performance and handling. What matters is how it makes me feel. This car poked me right in the fizz gland.

Excellent. I'm happy.

The joy of 600

There's a good chance you're reading this on a smart-phone or something like an iPad.[1] How fantastic is that? Forgive me for still being amazed by this sort of thing, but it is completely mind-blowing. I recently worked out that there's more processing power in my pocket today than there was in the whole country when I was born.

The internet: it's the greatest single advancement that humankind has enjoyed in my lifetime. The world's people and their thoughts are all within arm's reach, always. And it's perfectly accessible. A smartphone isn't bag-of-chips cheap, granted, but when its price is

---

[1] Not any more, obvs

measured against what it can do for you, nothing comes even remotely close. Not even chips. And these things are improving so quickly that your new one is outdated by the time you've finished unboxing it. It is the greatest triumph that manufacturing science has yet given us.

But not far behind, I'd like to suggest, is the 600cc sports motorcycle. Sports bikes have become unfashionable, usurped by adventure bikes and super scooters, but I don't think we should write them off just yet. The 600cc sports bike is, to my mind, the perfect consumer good, because everything about it – price, size, weight, performance, appearance, proportions, sound, usability, capacity, chassis technology – resolves at a sort of nodal point of motorcycle desirability that makes me fizz so fearsomely, I'm consumed by a baboon-like urge to mount it and be off. The gods will it.

Mine's a Honda CBR600RR, but that's a detail. Any offering from the Japanese big four, or Triumph, or the Italians, will do, and as long as it was built in the last decade, because these things haven't advanced that much owing to the decline in sales. They may disappear entirely soon – the CBR certainly will because Honda can't see the point in spending the cash to upgrade the engine to meet Euro 4 emissions laws. But no matter; I've already got mine and if I could get it up the stairs I'd keep it next to my side of the bed. You should have one too.

For the money – possibly only a couple of thousand pounds second-hand – no machine will tap into your sensory receptors like a 600cc sports bike. No boat, no car, no manky kit-built light aircraft. Its performance envelope is as crisply defined as the edge of a broken pane of glass viewed under a microscope, and it will respond to inputs – from the controls; from your mood even – so crisply and immediately that to say 'you almost wear this bike' would be a hackneyed disservice to the breed. You absorb a 600cc sports bike into the stuff of your being, and riding one is as endlessly astonishing and enduringly satisfying as having genitalia. I'd ride mine naked to wring every last ounce of man/machine interaction out of the relationship, but the gravel rash could be hideous.

Hang on, you may well be saying. Why not go the whole hog and have a litre-class bike? 'Why didn't you just buy a Fireblade?' is a question I'm often asked.

But a Fireblade, apart from being more expensive, is a deadly serious motorcycle. The CBR600RR is proper enough whilst remaining a toy, a divertissement; something that could be described as 'crafty' if it were a smoke, or 'cheeky' if it were a glass of wine at an inappropriate time of the day.

I'm also told, usually by bike journalists, that the shortcoming of the 600 class is that it has to be worked hard to give of its best. Is this an issue? We love the flexibility of a supercar engine after enduring the mealy-mouthed narrow rev range of a plodding diesel, so taking the Honda up to 15,000rpm is a delicious indulgence. And anyway, the bike journalists are wrong, and merely posturing. The CBR is brisk enough at low revs, really quite startling in the mid-range, and quite hard to compute beyond that. To be honest, on the few occasions I open it right out, I pretty much soil my German beer-drinking trousers.

But that's OK by me. It lets me know I'm still alive.

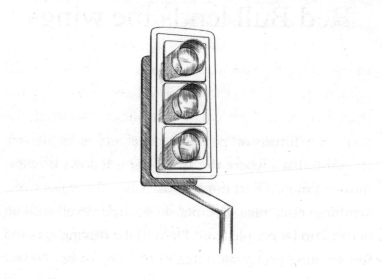

Red Bull lends me wings

Since the future of personal transport is in the air (because that's where the space is), it follows that the future of motorsport must be up there, too. Apart from anything else, race circuits at ground level will be booked up by people from DriveTribe driving cars for fun, because pretty soon that's not going to be allowed in the real world.

Air racing, then. It has a long and wreckage-strewn history as old as the aeroplane itself, which is getting on for 120 years if you haven't been paying attention. It has evolved from simple point-to-point competitions (think of *Those Magnificent Men in Their Flying Machines*) through terrifying multi-plane events around unforgiving wooden towers, to the form in which it is best known today, which is the Red Bull Air Races.

On the face of it, the Red Bull Air Races don't sound that promising. The aeroplanes race one at a time, against the clock, around a short course marked out with inflatable pylons, or 'air gates'. So there is no overtaking, no crashing into each other, and even the air gates are so gossamer thin that a plane can fly right through one in complete safety, the structure simply collapsing like a punctured ego. You do get a time penalty, though.

A Brazilian pilot, Adilson Kindlemann, did once end a race upside down in a river, although he was OK. Australian Matt Hall did better than this, by somehow flying into the drink but then recovering and flying out again. I'm not sure this has ever happened before. Overall, Red Bull Air Races have an unblemished safety record.

Dull? Now I've been to see the final of the 2018 series live, in Texas, I'd say definitely not. There are only two basic types of aeroplane in the championship, so they're all evenly matched. It's about pilot skill. You can see the whole course from any spectator spot, which is not true of any race circuit at zero feet QFE that I've ever been to. The planes are faster than F1 cars and fly at 15 metres above the deck, manoeuvring so violently that the pilots are subjected to 10g. And that's proper brain-draining g, not that snowflake lateral stuff.

More importantly, the aeroplanes are as colourful as exotic flowers and draw beautiful shapes in the sky, trailing smoke, so that the pilot's efforts are recorded as an aerial sketch that dissolves and then is gone, a bit like a Banksy.

And consider this: the last round, and indeed the whole championship, went down to the final run of the day. And even though there was only one aeroplane in the sky, I spotted the moment where Martin Šonka snatched victory.

The pilots have a day of practice and qualifying, as usual with motor racing. The difference is, though, that the circuit they learned on Saturday was not the one they fly on the Sunday; because on Saturday the weather was sunny and still, and on Sunday it was overcast and blustery. These things – air temperature, air pressure, wind speed and direction – affect the way aeroplanes fly and even how their engines run.

Šonka cracked it as he turned around air gate number 8. Flying aeroplanes is about managing energy, in the dullest possible terms, and he wasted not a drop of it in what looked, from the ground, like a perfect drifting stroke from a master calligrapher's pen. That was the win, right there, in the fraction of a second saved that put him on the top step of the podium.

Good to watch. I can't remember the last time I thought that about an F1 race.

All things uncomely
and broken . . .

So wrote W.B. Yeats. He must have been in a barn at the time.

If I were Richard Hammond, I'd be a bit worried. To be honest, if I were Richard Hammond, I'd be suicidal, because every day I'd wake up and realise I was Richard Hammond. Of more immediate concern, though, is that his birthday present is a mysterious 'barn find'.

Hammond is beside himself. He doesn't know what he's getting for his birthday from his fragrant and wonderful wife; he knows only that it's in a barn and will be revealed soon. How exciting is that? Well, hang on a minute.

Imagine if I said, 'Hammond, your birthday present

is going to be a big surprise. All I can tell you is that I found it in a wheelie bin round the back of a housing estate.'

Because that's what a barn find is. Assuming this is a real one, and not merely a tatty MG Midget that's been parked in a barn for effect, then it's something that's been thrown away. It's not as if, at the birth of Richard Hammond, someone said, 'Let's put this Birdcage Maserati in an old barn so that a gobby bloke from Birmingham can find it when he's thirty-eight.' No, whatever it is was put in a barn for the same reason that most of us put things in a skip. Because it was broken. It's just that people with barns have more space for crap and aren't obliged to take it to the dump.

I bought a barn find once. It was only a 90cc Honda step-through motorcycle and cost virtually nothing, but you could tell. That it was found in a barn, I mean. It was unadulterated tat from end to end, so I took it to the corporation tip, thereby completing a task that someone failed to get around to thirty years earlier.

I'm slightly surprised at Hammond, whom I regard as

an intelligent bloke. Living as he does in medieval England, he owns a barn. In it one may 'find' a selection of metal objects waiting to be turned into something useful, like a toaster. So he must know.

'What if . . . what if . . . ?' asks the Hamster in his own articles, under a picture of 50 per cent of a car that might have been driven by Clement Attlee. What if indeed. I'm assuming what he's going to find is a car, a bike, or possibly a tractor of some sort, but let's not be hasty. I've compiled a list of some of the other things that are found in old barns:

> Bat shit.
> Broken lawnmowers.
> Hay.
> Horses.
> Rusty barbecue.
> Some of a bicycle from before the war.
> A barn dance.
> Murder victims.

Barns, to people who live in the sticks, are like attics to the rest of us. It's where you put junk. It's why the

TV show *Cash in the Attic* doesn't work. There is no cash in the attic, only stuff that no one has put in the bin yet.

I can't wait to find out what it is.

Alpine must survive

It always annoys me when people say to me, 'If I were you, I'd . . . ,' because it makes no sense. If they were me, they'd be me, and doing whatever it is I'm doing that they don't approve of.

But if I were you, and you can, I'd buy an Alpine A110. If the company shuts down, as rumoured, you'll have a very rare car. If enough of you buy one, it will stay open, which is the result I'd like.

Here's why Alpine deserves to survive. As we all slowly come to accept that the future of driving will be electric in some form or other, there is another way worth considering, at least in the interim.

It's downsizing. This is considered an ethical and

moral thing to do in all aspects of our lives, and was a hot topic until recently, when it suddenly became one of those things that everyone's forgotten about, along with plastic in the ocean and *The Crown* on Netflix. But it's still there.

The Alpine is not, as many people suggest, a sports car. It is a downsized supercar. Of course the performance is more in the sports car league, but the sensations – and that's what matters – are pure supercar: engine buzzing behind you, front end going a bit frisky, gears bangin' through as you come out of the turn. It's tremendous.

All this, remember, from only 1.8 litres and four cylinders, which is exactly why a lot of people would dismiss it. But as I've said before, so many times that I'm boring myself, cars are not spreadsheets.

Low power inspired low weight and smaller size. This yielded better responses, not to mention lower consumption, lower emissions and lower insurance. The joy of driving a supercar has simply been reduced by around 30 per cent on a photocopier, and possibly enhanced in the process. It might be genius.

Obviously it's still not a cheap car, although it's less

than a third of the price of anything I've driven that gives comparable joy. The fuel consumption is not going to write any headlines of itself, but measured next to the level of indulgence, it's miraculous.

I really can't understand why this car hasn't been the roaring success that the original MX-5 was when it came out in my childhood, or even the Audi TT when the first one appeared. I've seen two others when I've been out in mine, and one of them was being driven by someone I knew.

Maybe it's because no one is trying it. You should. And then, if you can, you should buy one. The world will be a better place.

That's what I'd do, if I were you. Obviously.

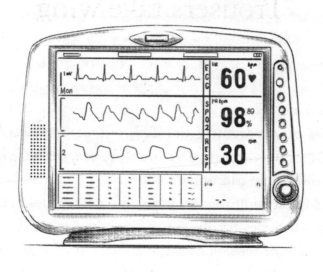

Trousers take wing

What do we want of the devices that empower our lives? Aesthetics first, I've often argued, because they are ultimately triumphant, and the story of humanity is told first and foremost in the way things look. That's why our hopes for the future are a 'vision'. There are no smells or sensations yet to come, but we can have a crack at what things might look like.

But since we have to interact with these devices, we want them to be pleasing in use, too. Doesn't matter whether it's a potato peeler or a yacht. Things that feel 'right', and balanced, reflect our inner desire for harmony and wellbeing. So in something like a car, art and technology combine, perhaps with a little psychology too, to provide resolution for our desires.

I hope that doesn't sound too pretentious. The point I wanted to make is that none of this involves a new jumper.

It's been bothering me for a while that Rolls-Royce Motor Cars, known generally simply as 'Rolls-Royce', now seem to be presenting themselves as 'House of Rolls-Royce'. What the hell are they on about? I've always rather liked Rolls-Royces, but I don't think I can drive one if everyone imagines I bought it from a stuffy department store where a liveried man in a brassy lift said, 'Third floor, alight for motor cars and sounding like an arse.'

And now a certain British sports-car maker from the middle of the country seems to have rebranded itself as Aston TK Maxxton. I'm reading about the Aston Martin by Hackett capsule collection, which has been inspired by a boat, thus deepening my confusion. It's a 22-piece collection (it says here) and includes outerwear, knitwear, shirts, polo shirts, trousers and accessories. What has happened? I'm forced to conclude that Aston, having run out of V-names for its cars, have moved on to the Aston Martin V-neck.

Stand-out pieces (their words again. I'd never say that) include the cobalt nautical parka. 'Its wind and waterproof qualities make it the perfect attire for driving the powerboat in any weather.' No shit, Sherlock. I expect Grace Darling knew that these were the qualities desirable in a boat jacket, and if you've got as far as owning a powerboat, you've probably worked out that you shouldn't wear a tweed waistcoat or a paper hazmat suit while driving it. And anyone in May's Britain who uses the word 'attire' will be going to prison. They'll be sharing a cell with someone who said 'beverage'.

'Key knitwear pieces include a cashmere half-zipped sweater in navy and grey and an insulating down-filled knit and merino wool sweater in navy with soft lambswool knitted sleeves and collar.'

Rubbish. What we want from you lot is auto-bloodymotive engibloodyneering.

Thank you.

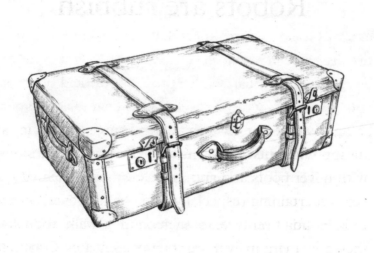

Robots are rubbish

Where we've got to with robots is one of the great disappointments in the history of technology, along with hover boots and anti-gravity. Honda's ASIMO is very entertaining (especially when he falls over), but it took Honda twenty years to get him to walk, and even then only marginally more convincingly than Clarkson does.

Recently, I've heard a lot of people saying things along the lines of, 'Well, the autonomous car is already here. My car can keep itself in its lane and at a constant distance from the car in front. It's just legislation stopping it.'

I've decided this is bollocks.

Yes, a lot of cars can do this radar cruise control and lane departure stuff. Teslas can do a lot more. But here's the problem. Driving cars is one of the most impressive and complex things humans do, and therefore a poor avenue down which to direct our robotic ambitions. Autonomous vacuum cleaners are much more realistic.

Driving a car, you deal with speeds we have not evolved to compute and extremities that are not truly sensed by us. There's also a huge amount going on around you that has to be dealt with. And yet, on the whole, we don't drive into each other or things. I know there are accidents, but compared with the number of vehicle movements, they're very rare.

Do we really think we are anywhere close to handing this sort of work over to robotics? The amount of information processing and sensory reception is enormous. So enormous, in fact, that I think we might move on from the car itself before the autonomous car happens.

Yes, a car that can 'keep station' on an unobstructed dual carriageway is with us, and that's no bad thing. But a truly autonomous car; one that allows you to sit in the back playing iPhone battleships while it drives itself through town? I refer you to the robot butler, which we thought we'd have by the 1980s.

Some years ago, I made a TV programme about robots. A German professor of all this stuff said to me, 'The most interesting thing about studying robotics is that we learn so much about people.' And what we're learning is that people are still brilliant.

Sorry.

That Beetle/911 clear-up

Since I wrote my piece on the 911 the other day, there have been, inevitably, several misinformed comments about the relationship between the 911 and the VW Beetle. So here, I hope, is some useful ammunition for future bar-room debates.

The 911 is not a glorified Beetle

If you want to be really smug here, you could point out that the first Beetles were, in fact, Porsches. Since the giant factory we now know as VW at Wolfsburg was still being built, the first few Beetles were built by Porsche in Stuttgart. I've driven one (number 6) and the original riveted plaque proclaiming as much is on the car. So you can stick that one in your rear compartment and go back to jokes about nuns having a spare engine in the boot/trunk.

Although Ferdinand Porsche did design the Beetle. Not Hitler

It was at Hitler's behest, sure, because the comedy dictator wanted an affordable car for the German workers to go with the affordable radio, affordable fridge, affordable cruises, cheap holidays, free concerts and community shouting. He is also believed to have said it should 'look like a beetle', because he thought that would make it perfectly streamlined.

Streamlining was da ting back then. But he gave the job of designing it to Porsche.

But that Ferdinand Porsche had nothing to do with the 911

Because he died twelve years before the 911 appeared. The 911 was the work of his grandson, Butzi Porsche. By then (1964), Porsche was a car manufacturer. Back in the 1930s, when Ferdinand senior was working on the Beetle, Porsche was a consultancy and builder of the occasional prototype.

They do seem suspiciously similar, though

When Ferdinand Sr designed the Beetle, he was really producing a sort of 'greatest hits' of contemporary small-car thinking. There were many 'people's car' projects on the go in the 1920s and 1930s, especially in Germany. Some of them (for Zündapp and NSU) had also been designed by Porsche. There were also cars by Hanomag (see the 2/10), Josef Ganz (see Standard Superior), Tatra (in Czechoslovakia), and others.

The thinking was that a small, air-cooled engine would be cheap to make, reliable and dependable. By putting it in the back, the drive to the wheels would be simplified and the interior space improved – no transmission tunnel. Not having an engine at the front would allow better aerodynamics. An engine at the back would bring less noise and stink into the interior.

This was the accepted logic and was openly discussed in the German technical automotive press. Porsche acknowledged the influence of other cars in his design for the Beetle.

Aspects of a broadly similar approach to a 'people's car' were later adopted by Fiat in Italy, Renault in France, Rootes in Britain, Zaporozhets in the Soviet Union and Mazda in Japan, to name just a few. But the problem for history is that this movement produced only two truly iconic cars: the Beetle and the Fiat 500. The rest are largely forgotten, giving the impression that a rear-engined car is a quirk. It isn't. It was once regarded as the way ahead.

Porsche don't exactly make 'people's cars'

No, they don't. Or do they? Post the Second World War, Porsche, now run by the second-generation Ferry Porsche, wanted to make its own sports car. After some more prototyping, the result was the 356. Materials being in short supply at the time, and since there was a healthy relationship with the reborn VW factory (Ferdinand Sr had been chairman of the board before being booted out by the Allies), the early 356 used the engine basics and some suspension bits from the Beetle. It's happened since, with the 914/4 (known as the 'VW Porsche') using a Beetle engine and the 924 using a VW group van engine.

When the time came to replace the ageing and underpowered 356, Porsche found itself still wedded to the air-cooled rear-engined thang. That was what they did, and to some extent it's what their devoted customers expected. Nobody thought the 911 would survive as long as it has – it was supposed to disappear in the mid-1970s with the dawn of the front-engined 928. But it's still here, completely changed from the original, but apparently an anachronism because of where the engine sits.

And therefore apparently related to the Beetle. But it isn't. Not really.

Handy pocket timeline thing

1 Ferdinand Porsche (1875–1951) oversaw the Beetle – launched 1938.
2 Ferry Porsche (1909–98) oversaw the 356 – launched 1948.
3 Butzi Porsche (1935–2012) oversaw the 911 – launched 1963.

The largely forgotten man who links them together is Erwin Komenda (1904–66), who ran Porsche's bodyworks between 1931 and 1966. He helped substantially with the design of all three cars mentioned above. So if it was anyone's fault, it was his.

Begone dull car

I would like to try a 'thought experiment'; that is, one that can't be conducted in reality because it's a bit hypothetical, but with which we can wrestle in the dark recesses of the mind. A bit like that thing Einstein did with the clocks.

It involves removing a significant British car from our subconscious and trying to imagine if it would make any difference. This is deeply conceptual stuff, because certain cars are so rooted in our imagined sense of identity (Foreigners will have to bear with us on this. It's your own fault for being one.) that we assume to take them away would be a bit like removing the word 'sorry' from the language.

The difficulty lies in choosing the car, and it can't be anything too traumatic. So not the E-type Jag (Enzo Ferrari said it was the most beautiful, etc. etc.), not the Mini (Twiggy, *The Italian Job*, blah blah), not Bond's Aston DB5 (It will leave you shaken, but not stirred! LOL.) and not Captain Birkin's Blower Bloody Bentley (the supercharger is that bit sticking out at the front, you know). They're all a bit too embedded. It would be a bit like lamping a Beefeater.

I had in mind something more humble and workaday. Something we may not have noticed was important to us. I've settled on the Morris Minor, a flawed car (it should have been front-wheel drive with a flat-four engine) but one that is apparently dear to us. Even now, someone, somewhere, is saying, 'My grandma had one of those. It was an estate. It had real wood on the outside!'

Now the Morris Minor has gone. All surviving examples have been cubed and recycled as domestic appliances. The old ads have gone in the shredder. It's been bitmapped out of all the period TV dramas, where it was being driven by a nurse or an aspiring artist. The one in the Metropolitan Police Museum of

Panda Cars (I'm sure there is such a thing) has been buried in concrete at the footing of a new bridge. As Lt-Commander Thomas Woodrooffe said in his famous drunken commentary of the 1937 Coronation Review of the Fleet, it has gone, disappeared and gone. Let aeroplanes circle, moaning overhead, scribbling on the sky the message, it is dead.

Now: does it matter?

Bike theft – solved

I've now spent several hours digesting some crucial data on motorcycle theft. I felt it was important not to rush into a response.

As someone who loves motorcycles, it's an emotive issue; as someone whose new Triumph was badly damaged by thieves a few years ago, I find the idea that these gangs are brazenly roaming the streets, unchallenged, to be infuriating. Of course I do.

But the landscape of crime is never as simple as it seems. It's all too easy to believe that a zero tolerance crackdown in the community with greater powers and funding for law enforcement agencies (blah blah, whatever it is people say on radio phone-ins) is the right thing to say here. But I don't think it is. I think we need to address the root of the problem. I think we have to kill them.

It makes me shudder to write that. Like any civilised person, I am vehemently opposed to capital punishment and any other form of state-sponsored murder. Justice should not admit a public's thirst for pure revenge. But that's not what's happening here. I have arrived at this conclusion not through knee-jerk reaction or impotent fury, but by a pure and unadulterated process of logic. I think they have to be killed.

As the law-abiding public, we are not permitted to take the law into our own hands. I'm not suggesting we do. The law already exists, viz. it's wrong to steal motorcycles. It's simply that the law isn't being enforced. The police seem unwilling or in some way unempowered to deal with it, and the aggrieved people are unable to convene courts to try the perpetrators even if they could be caught, so they'll just have to be killed. That way, they won't nick any more bikes.

There is, as ever, the matter of morality to deal with. Many people imagine that theft is a cut-and-dried issue as far as morality is concerned, but this isn't so.

The 'ethics of burglary' is a subject worthy of debate because, let's be clear, there comes a point within the disparity of wealth and personal circumstance of peoples where it is entirely reasonable. It's what the Littleport Riots of 1816 were all about.

I hate the idea of people nicking my stuff, but in all honesty, I'm pretty well off. If a genuinely desperate man on his last gasp nicks my coat from the pub on a freezing night, well, he's welcome to it. It'll change his life, mine's only inconvenienced by having to buy another one. Even a truly desperate drug addict can have my coat. He's made a mistake somewhere in life and I haven't, which is my good fortune. But the people we're talking about here are just wankers nicking bikes for profit, so we should kill them.

It has, like *The Archers*, gone on long enough. What many assume is a spate of petty theft is in fact a threat to societal stability. These thieves are not merely taking other people's property, they are threatening anyone who opposes them with power tools, machetes and medieval debonkers. As several people have already pointed out, someone is going to be killed.

In which case, it might as well be them.

Reviewed: being nice

My English teacher used to say that 'nice' is a feeble word. Its use meant you couldn't really form a proper opinion, or find a better way of articulating the one you had.

She may have had a point. Anyone described as 'nice' is generally assumed to be a bit dull. People talk about a nice bit o' beef and have a nice sit down, and those people, you sense, are not greatly moved by the experience of being human. Ironically, the word 'nice' is a bit meh.

But none of this is true when it comes to cars. I've sat in presentations by motor industry marketing types, and they often have big clouds full of words that have supposedly guided the designers and engineers in the conception of their latest thing; they will be words such as 'premium' and 'exclusive', or even 'inviting' or maybe 'dynamic'. But never 'nice'. Nice is too difficult.

Plenty of cars are good but not particularly nice. The Audi R8 is one such, at least for me. I think it's excellent. I just don't find it very nice. The Kia Picanto GT-Line is nice, even though some bits of the interior are unpleasant. Am I making sense? I'm going to keep going anyway.

This BMW 440i is very nice. I'm rather partial towards mid-size BMW saloons and coupés anyway, because I find them tasteful and reassuringly German. This one is also nice, which is tremendous.

Why is it nice? Search me, but it is. It's a bit of an old model now, and there are a few things to criticise. In some circumstances, the ride can feel a bit nuggety. The writing on the buttons is too small. Eight gears sometimes feels like too many, and when the gearbox is trying to be clever, it can introduce what feels like an unnecessary downshift (the Rolls-Royce Dawn does this as well). It doesn't matter how good the gear changes are, not changing gear always feels better. But, bloody hell, it's nice. Really nice.

An especially nice feature, which you will notice as you walk towards it from the front three-quarters, is the shape of the rear wing. I can't explain it, really, but it makes my heart ache like Sir Thomas Wyatt's when he heard a naked foot in his chamber. My car is a particularly nice dark blue, but I haven't been able to photograph this bit successfully because the weather's so crap. Still, it's the nicest thing I've seen all day, except for our PA Kate's face, because she's just brought me a nice cup o' tea.

It's tempting to say, 'I wish all cars could be this nice,' but I won't, because then none of them would be nice; they'd all be normal. We need only a few cars to be truly nice, so that they can shine; so that if we took these cars away, the Renault Captur would seem nice.

And that would be awful.

Total bullshirt

There's a generally understood rule of cars that says anyone wearing a Ferrari hat doesn't own a Ferrari. At least, I hope they don't, since I actually do own a Ferrari and if some of the Ferrari hat-wearing people I've met also have one, I'll have to throw mine in the river. Jeez.

On the other hand, I often wear a T-shirt that says 'Honda 500' on it, and I do own a 500cc Honda (a 1972 CB500 Four, if anyone's interested). Somehow, this is acceptable. Why?

This is a thorny problem to which I gave a lot of thought the other day, as I was sitting in my Jacuzzi. I think I may have the answer.

Only other motorcyclists have a view on bikes, and

anyone who has a bike must be an enthusiast. You wouldn't have one otherwise. To everyone else they are entirely meaningless. So if I wear my Honda T, I'm talking only to the fraternity. A man or woman coming the other way might – at most – look at it and think, *Interesting. I have a Ducati myself.* It doesn't really go any further than that.

That tailored Lamborghini paddock jacket, meanwhile, makes you look a right tit. Because everyone knows about cars, understands the socio/political implications of car ownership, and recognises that supercars are owned by vulgarians, so they're going to take a view; viz. either that you do own a Lamborghini, and therefore own a supercar, and are *ipso facto* a tosser, or that you don't own a Lamborghini but have bought the jacket, and are therefore a charlatan.

So either way, you can't wear car-branded apparel (as it would be called in the brochure). So there's an end to that.

But I wasn't entirely happy with this theory, so I got back in the Jacuzzi, but this time with a bottle of something from 1970s France that I found kicking around in the basement, and had another go.

And after a while I thought to myself, *May, you're talking total crap*. Because if you own a reasonable car, such as a Toyota Aygo, why not wear it with pride? Or a deep show of irony, if it's the VW Jetta? My mum owns and loves a Suzuki Splash, and no one can hold that against her, so she should enjoy it in the form of a decorated raincoat as well.

In fact, we should all do it. Have your car on a shirt, hat, umbrella or stylish slimline document case. Your car, apparently, says something about you. Say it again, with fashion. Car badges are, after all, cool bits of very considered design. Rolls-Royce T-shirt, Dacia T-shirt, Mitsubishi T-shirt – great. Let's do it.

This still, however, leaves me with a problem. And the problem isn't car-branded clothing, it's supercars.

I mean, in my vision of the future, everyone else will have their cars on their chests, but I can't do that for the reasons outlined in paragraph one. There will therefore come a time when someone sees me and thinks, *That bloke isn't wearing his car brand on his T-shirt. That must mean he has a Ferrari.*

What a twat.

Mein Porsche ist kaputt

Every now and then there will be a story in a classic car magazine about how someone has found a Lamborghini or the like that's been sitting forgotten in a garage for forty years.

I'm always amazed. I might forget that I own a disposable ballpoint pen, but I couldn't forget that I had a garage with a supercar in it.

But now I know how it happens. There's my 911, parked in my secret underground bunker, where I left it a few weeks ago. It won't unlock when I press the button on the key, but that's normal. After a couple of days of no use, the 911 goes into a sort of shut-down mode to preserve the battery. All you do is put the key into the lock, give it half a turn, and it wakes up again. Then it unlocks with the plipper, and you can be on your way.

But this time it didn't.

It has happened before; a few months back, when the car's original battery failed. I couldn't even open the front luggage lid to jump start it, because it's electric. There is an alternative way to open the lid using a booster pack attached to a stupid little pull-out pin in the fuse box, which is in the front footwell, but that means opening the door.

So I unlocked the door manually and opened it. And then the alarm went off, which surprised me, since the battery was flat. The sound of a Porsche alarm going off in an enclosed and echoing space is like passing your own head through a bandsaw, but I struggled on and opened the front lid, then disconnected one of the battery leads. The alarm stopped.

But then it started again, obvs, and my ears caved in.

After a few minutes it stopped again, just long enough for the sepulchral silence of the cool subterranean car storage facility to imbue me with a deep sense of calm. But then it started again. And then it stopped. And then started again, and so it went on, until I was driven into a corner, where I crouched down, gibbering, with a bucket on my head.

After about half an hour, but which felt like all of my life up until that point, the alarm stopped completely. I bought a new battery, wired it all up, and the car came to life and worked as it should.

But now . . . I'm not exaggerating when I say I'm too scared to open the door, because the noise of the alarm has been reserved in hell as a punishment for people who serve food on pieces of wood, it's that bad.

I can't take a recovery truck down there, because it won't fit through the door. I can't push it out of the bunker, because I parked it in gear, so I'd have to unlock the door manually and open it, and the alarm will go off. I could call the local Porsche garage and they would send a man out. But what's he going to do? He'll have to open the door, and we'll all be killed. I have another car. I'll use that.

Let's fast-forward to 2050, when a man from *Classic Piston Sportscar* writes a story about how this mint

2010 Porsche 911 with under 30,000 miles on the clock has been found in a bunker in London. How did that happen?

Here's how.

The great British not-to-takeaway

Where would you find a burger van? In a lay-by, usually, maybe announced a mile before by a piece of cardboard propped up by the road with the legend 'OPEN' on it, in crayon.

Burger vans are places we go to, or that draw us in like sizzling sirens, when we were meaning to go somewhere else. They don't come to us. They are mobile yet strangely permanent, like navigational waypoints, distance markers or menhirs connecting us to the Earth's positive energy paths. They also do sausage sandwiches.

Almost fifteen years ago, Jeremy Clarkson and I were involved in a film shoot at a race circuit, and one of the props we needed was a burger van. A researcher duly rustled one up, and there it was, by the side of the track. It was even operational. I had a fried egg sanger.

How did he do that? Organise a burger van, I mean. We admitted at the time that we wouldn't have a clue where to start. We could arrange to borrow cars, we could suggest locations, we could probably even drum up some people to dress up as Roman soldiers. But a burger van?

In the years since, in quiet moments, I've often returned to the quandary. May, quick, arrange a burger van for tomorrow. How?

Now, obviously, there are organisations that hire out props for film and TV. They can do all sorts of things. Entire period office interiors, Stormtroopers and every costume imaginable. I've been to a number of these places. I've never seen a burger van.

It's more difficult than it sounds. You could drive to a burger van you knew and ask the bloke with the spatula if he'd like to bring his van to a racetrack for the day. How much? Well, you'd have to pay him what he'd earn in his lay-by on the same day, and a good van can turn over a lot of money. We don't want a crap one.

Plus, there would be the cost of moving it, which would be significant, because a lot of these things haven't moved for decades. They have grown into the ground and acquired an archipelago of plastic furniture, bins and sauce bottles. That would all have to be moved.

And he still wouldn't agree to it. An empty lay-by invites annexation by a rival, and regular customers would be disappointed by the absence of their usual burger. That could have a long-term effect, because the clientele might try another van and prefer it. So burger man would need a comprehensive publicity campaign to make it clear that he was only gone for the day. That sort of thing costs a bloody fortune.

So that approach doesn't work. It would be far too expensive for a 15-second TV exchange that happened to have a burger van in the background. I'd have to find someone with a burger van who wasn't using it.

That van simply can't exist. No one would have a fully functioning burger van but not use it. That's bad business, and burger vannery is pure business. Burger vans are not collectors' items, which is why there isn't one in the National Motor Museum. If you weren't using it, you'd sell it, and the person who bought it would be someone who was going to use it for an enabling burger-based roadside solutions enterprise. So it's in a lay-by, doing business, and we're back where we started.

Well, look. Normally, if we need something a bit left field, like a Winnebago or a JCB, we just ring up the people who make them, grovel a bit and borrow it. So why not do the same with a burger van, eh?

Because as far as I can make out, no one actually makes a burger van as I would understand one. They evolve from other things – caravans, camper vans, Transits. I've even seen one fashioned from an old container on the back of a flatbed. All burger vans are very old and studied by students of medieval history, looking for evidence that nomadic Danes brought their knowledge of bread rolls to these islands. You cannot build a true burger van any more than you could build the remains of an Iron Age settlement.

So I'm stumped. I need a burger van, tomorrow. Whichever researcher managed that last time deserves the Victoria Cross.

A car clichés quiz

As a car enthusiast, how predictable are you? Each car listed below sparks a particular and immediate reaction whenever it's mentioned. But do you know what it is?

Reliant Scimitar

1) Princess Anne had one of those, you know.
2) Princess Margaret had one of those, you know.
3) Princess Grace of Monaco had one of those, you know.
4) Prince had one of those, you know.

Honda NSX

1) NSX meant 'Ayrton Senna' in Japanese, you know.

2) Ayrton Senna had nothing to do with the NSX, you know.

3) That was developed by Ayrton Senna, you know.

4) Ayrton Senna had never heard of the Honda NSX, you know.

Austin Allegro

1) Austin Allegro was the name of a BL security guard, you know.

2) The Austin Allegro was heavier upside down than it was the right way up, you know.

3) The Austin Allegro was more aerodynamic in reverse than it was going forwards, you know.

4) The Austin Allegro cost more in beige, you know.

McLaren F1

1) The engine bay is lined in lead, you know.

2) The engine bay is lined in real gold, you know.

3) The engine bay is lined in Terry's All Gold, you know.

4) The CD player will only play Spandau Ballet's 'Gold', you know.

Any Peugeot

1) They also make pepper spray, you know.

2) They also make Peperami, you know.

3) They also make pepper grinders, you know.

4) They're also on Grindr, you know.

Any Rolls-Royce

1) The loudest noise inside is the tocking of the clock, you know.

2) The loudest noise inside is the inexorable linearity of time's arrow, you know.

3) The loudest noise inside is the teachings of The Rock, you know.

4) The loudest noise inside is the ticking of the clock, you know.

Any Lamborghini

1) They started out making tracksuits, you know.

2) They started out making biblical tracts, you know.

3) They started out making tractors, you know.

4) They started out making Tic Tacs, you know.

Any old Fiat

1) They had a factory on the roof of their test track, you know.
2) They had a roof on their test-track factory, you know.
3) They had a test track on the roof of their factory, you know.
4) They killed JFK, you know.

Morgan Plus 6

1) They're made in the woods, you know.
2) The engine is made of wood, you know.
3) The chassis is made by Edward Woodward, you know.
4) The chassis is made of wood, you know.

SAAB 99

1) They also made fighter jets, you know.
2) They also made 'Benny and the Jets', you know.
3) They also made 'Jet', by Wings, you know.
4) They also made Jet from Gladiators, you know.

Cars and truth

Richard Hammond and I have often indulged in a lengthy and drunken debate at the end of which we conclude that 95 per cent of everything is rubbish.

This actually stands up surprisingly well. History has bequeathed very little to us, compared with what it produced, so all the wooden furniture, computer coding, watercolour portraiture and curry recipes that went in the bin must have been a bit sub-optimal, or we'd still have them.

Think how many books have been printed and Kindle files uploaded. It's an unimaginable number, and most of them have been converted into bog roll (or the digital equivalent) because they were rubbish. I know this for sure, because I've been responsible for some of them.

The '95 per cent' theory is very robust, but even so, I've decided to revise it. I now think that 95 per cent of everything is untrue. A fiction, of sorts.

Let's take art – always a contentious one. At the apogee of the art pyramid, we might find The Truth. This is why truly fabulous art is a priceless commodity; it represents what we seek better than anything else, and is in obviously finite supply. But the rest of art is little more than a trick, a technique for duping your brain into thinking that Ted Nugent, the offspring of a virgin, is really there on the wall, or page.

Now I think about it, much of what we believe to be the universal glue of the human condition is a myth, and really only stuff we've agreed to agree on. The value of diamonds, for example; complete bollocks, and merely part of a belief system. In reality, rice and potatoes are much more valuable, for which would we rather do without, for ever? Nationhood, political theories, economic systems, religions, brand loyalties – maybe they're just all convenient above everything else. They're not real.

So where does this leave cars, 95 per cent of which will be forgotten? I've often argued that the most important attribute of a car is the way it looks, because when its relevance as a transport commodity has been exhausted, it might still (if it's good enough) earn a lowly place in that pyramid of art we met earlier and become a part of the history of how things looked.

But in the moment, what we love about cars is the way that driving them feels. We imagine that it's an emotional response, but in reality it's down to physics. Physics, ironically enough, is full of so-called 'fictional forces', the centrifugal one being an example, and the one that thrills us in corners. But physics on the whole is perfectly true, and was the first thing to exist. And if a modern, sentient human being could be transported back to the cataclysmic big bang that began everything, acceleration would feel the same as it does now.

Our love of cars is quite literally a gut reaction; a direct communion with the purest and most steadfast truth we know. But always remember that, perforce, 95 per cent of everything I've just said must be crap.

Reviewed: Italian

Most English-speaking car enthusiasts will know that the German term for a sports exhaust is 'sportauspuff'. That's funny, but in Italian it's a 'scarico sportivo', so I know which country I'd rather have been born in if I ran the local Kwik Fit.

Italian – it sounds good. It may sound perfectly normal if you are Italian, in the way that Indian food, if you're Indian, is simply 'food'. To the rest of us, though, it makes everything a bit more exciting.

This morning, for example, I was rooting around on some Ferrari dealers' websites and came across a rather gorgeous 308 GTB Vetroresina. This version, an early car, is worth a 50 per cent premium over a later steel-bodied 308. But hang on a minute.

'Gran tourismo berlinetta vetroresina' means 'hard-top glass-fibre'. You're paying an extra 50 grand or so to be able to say, 'I've got the plastic Ferrari.' It's made out of the same stuff as a canoe, it's only that Ferrari has a nicer way of putting it.

Let's consider that most celebrated of Italian super-cars, the original Lamborghini Countach; or, to use its full name, the Lamborghini Countach Longitudinale Posteriore Quattrocento Periscopo. In English, that's the Lamborghini Wowzers Lengthways Up The Arse Four Hundred Silly Mirror. And while we're at it, the Ferrari Testarossa translates as the Ginger Blacksmith.

'Maserati' is a lovely word to say, and so is 'Quattroporte'. The equivalent car from the British Midlands would have been the Morris Four-Door. Rubbish. The British Midlands did produce the Triumph Acclaim, and legend has it that it never sold in Germany because its name translates as 'Sieg Heil'. I've always doubted this, so checked with a German mate. 'It is impossible to translate Sieg Heil,' he confirmed.

In Italian, however, it's the Acclamazione di Trionfo, which sounds nothing like a second-rate, licence-built Honda saloon. America's AMC Pacer becomes the Battistrada, the Works Limited Edition of the Mini Cooper becomes the Lavora in Edizione Limitata, and even the Morris Ital is better in Italian, because it's the Morris Italiano. The only British car that doesn't benefit from translation is the Ford Cortina. Because that's already Italian.

It's where the British motor industry went wrong. Take the Reliant Robin. It's a plastic three-wheeler named after a boring bird. In Italian, it's the Tre Ruota Vetroresina Pettirosso.

And now you want one.

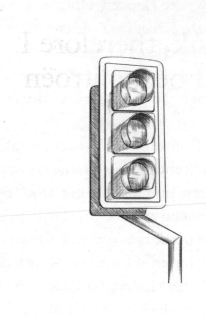

I think, therefore I must be a Citroën

René Descartes, a Frenchman who spent much of the seventeenth century sitting on a bar stool thinking about whether or not he was, reckoned that the human soul dwelt in a part of the brain called the pineal gland.

This was pretty convenient, in a way, since Descartes was wrestling with the Mechanical Philosophy worldview, so locating something as inexplicable as the soul in a tiny place in the middle of your head saved him the bother of having to explain it.

Meanwhile, elsewhere on DriveTribe, some people have been headbutting that old chestnut of whether or not a car has a soul. Well, I don't want to sound like a mardy old sod, but no, it doesn't. In fact, I think that attributing the appeal of a car to its 'soul' is a bit lazy, as it excuses you (see René, above) from having to explain it.[2]

Machine character, though; that's something else, and it's very much apparent. There's usually a lot of it in a complex machine, such as a car or motorcycle, even if it declares itself to be a bit of a dullard. That's still a characteristic. It can be found in simple things, as well. I have a special tin opener at home that definitely converses with me when I use it. My petrol lawnmower has a ton of character. It's a complete bastard.

I believe I have a soul, whatever that is, and so does my cat, as a living creature. He may, in fact, and in accordance with Hinduism, be the current host of the constantly migrating soul of Abraham Lincoln. Or he may simply have the one-off soul of a furry little fugger. Not my car, though. It has no soul.

I know I've said it before, but here it is again. The remarkable thing about cars is that they reveal the soul of humanity. That's much more interesting.

---

[2] I appreciate that I'm being a bit loose with my interpretation of Descartes's writing on his gland idea.

Man buys motorcycle

It was quite a difficult thing to do, so I thought I'd share it with you all in the hope that you'll reassure me. That I did the right thing. Or call me an arse, I don't really mind.

In effect, I've taken four nice bikes from my modest stable and swapped them all for one, and it's an oldie at that. It's a 1969 Honda CB750 'sandcast', and represents (as much as one motorcycle can) the dawn of the Japanese superbike.

The CB750 arrived in 1969, and before full production tooling was ready. Eventually, the engine cases would be pressure die-cast, but the first 7414 (of 550,000-odd) bikes were produced with so-called 'sandcast' cases.

This is a misnomer, in fact. The engine cases were not traditionally cast in sand, but by the 'permanent mould' gravity process, which is similar to die-casting but using – get this – gravity instead of pressure to fill the mould. There are metallurgical and productivity pros and cons to both methods, but the important difference to motorcycle bores is that the cases of these early bikes look rougher than the fully tooled-up version, and mark them out as rare and exclusive.

Mine has a number in the 4000s, making it quite soon after the big bang of the big Japanese bike. I have now joined an odd global fraternity of early CB750 enthusiasts, who will spend many hours on forums and at meetings discussing very fine points of authenticity.

But what we are really doing is saying to other CB750 owners, 'Yes, I've got one of those too, but I paid up to ten times as much as you did because I wanted the shit-looking engine.'

If you do happen to be a CB750 nerd, then yes to the correct front mudguard; and yes to the right wheel rims; and to the master cylinder, the brake caliper, the airbox, the throttle linkage, the number of screws in the clutch cover, and everything else that marks this out as a slightly inferior version of a truly historic motorcycle, although in fairness at a much higher price.

And yes, just pop round if you fancy a go.

Jus' kiddin'!!!!!!!!

I'm a Celerio

This year has definitely had wheels on it. I've driven no end of interesting cars all over the world, ridden motor-cycles, dabbled further in electric motoring, built a bicycle from bits, and bought a lawnmower (the roller of which counts). I even won a wheelbarrow in a summer fête raffle. It's the only prize I've ever won, but at least it, too, has a wheel.

Meanwhile, one of the most memorable drives of the year came right at its start; memorable because it revealed a shortcoming in me. And I'm afraid it was in a 1.0-litre Suzuki Celerio. My 140-character Twitter road test of the time said: 'Surprisingly thrashable with amusing engine and low costs, let down by dreary interior door panels.' I was right. The interior door panels on the Celerio are really low rent. But let's look into this a bit further.

Now I don't want to revisit that tiresome old chestnut about how small and underpowered cars are more fun more of the time, simply because you have to work them harder and understand their limits more completely than you do those of an excessively endowed road rocket. There, I've done it. So let's move on.

The route was the one I take regularly. Just under 100 miles, and a mixture of town, motorway, sweeping A-roads and, at the end, 12 miles of winding country lanes two peasants wide, with bends badly engineered under Richard the Lionheart, blind crests, stray dinosaurs, all that sort of stuff. It's a great test route for any car, but it's that last bit that is perhaps most revealing. This is where my 458 is slow, and a car like the Celerio sets records. Of the Celerio, *What Car* says, 'The performance is better suited to town driving.' Bollocks it is.

In fact, the Celerio made an interesting comparison with the May household's general-purpose biffabout, a

Fiat Panda Pop. It was all about engines. Japan gives us a 1.0-litre three-pot, Italy a 1.2-litre four. Peak power, I happened to know, was about the same for both, and neck-snapping at that. A tad under 70bhp.

But torque delivery was the real issue, as it generally is. Logic says that, other things being equal, the three-cylinder would produce a bit more lower down, whereas the four would be more willing to rev. And so it seemed. At certain well-worn parts of my test route – for example, a bit where you round a tight, off-camber right-hander and are then confronted with a steep climb – the Suzook seemed to ace it, ever so slightly. We're talking about marginal differences here, but real connectivity in a car is about the resolution of the dynamic information being downloaded to your sensory receptors. Small, simple cars are very well connected. I could feel the difference. The Japanese motor would hunker down like a weightlifter at the absolute limit of his lifting power, and throb a bit.

No need to look up the figures for this stuff. Everything you need to know is in your bones. I often think I can sense this stuff in my kneecaps, for some reason. The Fiat could be wrung out a bit more and seemed to enjoy it, but the Zooki had a smidge more grunt in its bowels. It would all be to do with stroke length, crank angles and other stuff inherent in the two engines' basic configurations: three pots versus four pots. Again, there's no need to get bogged down in it. Your very viscera knows it, instinctively.

Well, it goes to show, once again, that driving, like music, is a performative experience. It's all about sensations and perception, not absolutes. Out of interest, I looked up the official figures, and they are thus: Suzuki, 66lb ft at 3500rpm; Fiat, 75lb ft at 3000rpm. I know the Panda is a heavier car, and that has a huge bearing on all this, but I was still convinced of the Suzuki's superior low-range torque.

So there you go. Lesson learned. My arse dynamometer is rubbish.

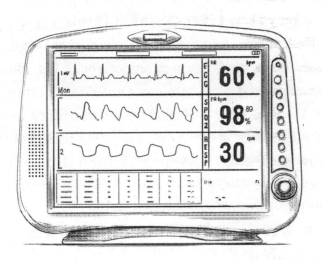

The road test of the century

The car that was to be my hot ride for series three of *The Grand Tour* was the new Toyota Century. But it's not to be, because the car won't be available over here in time to film it, so whatever the Century has to offer is somewhere in the future.

I'm gutted, frankly. What a car this must be. The Century (I realise the sentence is going to sound confusing) has been around since 1967, and has generally evolved quite gently. This one, though, is a radical update, with hybrid V8 power (it used to have a V12), more space, active noise suppression and new styling lending it 'an air of dignity and excellence'. The shape of the doors is inspired by the design of room partitions from Japan's Heian period (it says here).

Ironically, given that Toyota pioneered the mass-manufacturing system by which most significant goods are now made, the Century is hand-built, and at a rate of just fifty a month. You must remember that the rest of the Toyota empire can produce a transporter-load of cars in the time it takes you to eat a bowl of Sugar Puffs.

This is different. It's built by the sort of Japanese craft types who undoubtedly spent the first thirty years of their apprenticeships learning to sharpen a chisel. The Phoenix badge alone takes six weeks to engrave by someone with a very steady hand and either fantastic eyesight or incredible reading specs.

Heads of state and captains of industry ride in the reclining left-hand rear seat, which is where all the best people sit in cars, including Richard Hammond. That's where I was hoping to be, but alas, no.

Later this century, perhaps.

Why I like the Civic Type R

There are a number of things I would criticise about the Honda Civic Type R. I find the engine a bit coarse at low revs and the power delivery a bit sudden. The interior is rather ordinary and pressing the R button simply spoils the whole car: the ride, the steering feel. It's like having a 'wings ice up' button on your aeroplane seat. Everything suddenly becomes much worse.

There's also the simple fact that it's about to be replaced, even though it only seemed to arrive – finally – about a month ago.

But what's really bothering me about the Civic Type R is the way it looks. I think it looks absolutely terrific, but Pinky and Perky disagree. They think it looks awful, and prefer the Golf GTI, because they're well cubic.

I think we should take a moment to remind ourselves what a hot hatch is for, which is first and foremost to look a bit ridiculous. The Civic looks really silly and a bit like some flying cars I drew in the back of my maths exercise book. But it also looks fantastic, full of surprising angles and weird interpenetrations. Plus those winglet things. If you drive that, you are a serious helmsman. Or you might be a right yobbo. But either way, it's better than pretending your focused performance tool is really an ordinary hatchback.

For years my main criticism of Japanese cars in general was that they didn't look very Japanese. They just looked like cars. But the Type R does. I can't explain *why* it does, but you know it isn't European, it definitely isn't American, and it can't possibly be a Hyundai. In fact, it's definitely a performance Honda. I think it looks tremendous, and it makes me fizz and laugh in equal measure.

But even Jethro Bovingdon (late of DriveTribe) is unconvinced by the 'styling'. For some reason he believes it's a good car, whereas I think it's a faintly aggravating car that I would still have because of the way it looks. What is wrong with everyone? The Civic Type R is terrific.

Am I alone in this? Since what amount to elaborate surveys can now decide things like the independence of whole nations, I'm prepared to put it to the vote.

Please read the following statement and tick the box that most closely corresponds with your own view.

The Civic Type R looks totally epic.

☐   Yes, I agree. It's properly tidy.
☐   I am a dullard.

Your executive toolkit
has arrived

I'm inclined to think that a reet posh tool bag is for tools who have tools that aren't ever going to be used. But maybe that's the predictable reaction of an embittered man who fears the misappropriation of artisanal essentials for the purpose of making hopeless people feel better. Maybe what we have here is just part of society's long and agonising death by luxury goods.

I have before me a picture of an automotive toolkit, car-themed, hence the accelerator pedal zip pulls. It's made using Connolly leather by Sebastian Conran, and is part of the 'Pit Stop' collection. Also available are a ladies' beauty case, a jump-leads case [*sic*], CD case and pet carrier. Not yet available is a case for a cocked and loaded Webley revolver so you can do yourself in swiftly and mercifully when you realise what a total tosser you've become.

No, that's not fair. Why not apply to the tool case the care and respect afforded a fine handbag or document case? Here it is, probably very aromatic. There are some very nice Facom fast-action combination spanners in there; I use those. (Mine live in a plastic box.)

However. Sebastian, me old mate, you've included an adjustable in there. Nothing screams not-actually-a-mechanic like one of those, the tool of the charlatan. Kindly chuck that in the river and replace with Facom item 83SH.JP9, 9-piece metric ball-ended hex key set.

Cheers.

Man sells car

If you've read car magazines for as long as I have, you will have at some point – probably about once every year – come across the 'XXX for Mondeo money' story.

It goes like this: for the money you were going to spend on your dreary mainstream Mondeo, you could have an old Porsche 911/Lamborghini/tatty Ferrari or whatever (fill in your own XXX). Be different. Express your credentials as a true motoring enthusiast and not just a sheep-like consumer.

I've always been dismissive of this idea. The best car to buy for Mondeo money is, in fact, a Mondeo, especially if you need a car in the accepted car-like role of dependable transport. And since you were looking at a Mondeo, that's probably exactly what you were after. Not a Urraco.

And anyway, it's not true. About eight years ago, I bought a mainstream air-cooled 911 for a bit less than Mondeo money, but last year sold it for three times what I paid for it. Ha! A profit, something I've never achieved before.

And now I've decided that my 1972 Rolls-Royce Corniche has to go, because I've become allergic to it. And I mean this. If I drive it for more than half an hour, I start itching and then have to boil all my clothes. So it's going into an auction next month (Bonhams, at Goodwood) and it's expected to fetch one and a half times what I paid for it. Maybe twice.

So I'd like to apologise. Here were two cars bang in the for-Mondeo-money heartland, I did buy them and they haven't cost me anything to own. They were right, those misty-eyed car journalists, but they're not right any more, because all of these 'bargain exotics' (think, indeed, of the Urraco, Ferrari Dino 308 and Maserati Khamsin we drove on the telly years ago) are now worth much more than a Mondeo, and it's because of people like me. And Richard Hammond.

On the plus side, it does give Ford an excellent marketing opportunity as it launches its new Mondeo Vignale. 'A Mondeo for the price of a stupid old car. Two Mondeos, in fact.'

You're welcome.

Dacia cures cancer

The new Dacia Sandero has come top – which actually means bottom – in the latest cap hpi cost-of-ownership survey. What this means is that the basic Sandero 1.0 SCe Access is the absolute entry point for new car ownership, the thing at the infinitely narrow point of the inverted pyramid of possible fiscal commitment to motoring. It works out at £206.10 per month for the first three years.

For that, you get an entire motor car, which makes the Sandero compare favourably with the much more expensive but incomplete Ariel Atom, or the hideously expensive Lamborghini Huracan, which has only two seats.

To put this into perspective, a British smoker need give up only thirteen cigarettes a day to be rewarded with not only improved health but also a new car, along with the knowledge that he or she will – possibly – be relieving the burden on the National Health Service during these difficult times. People with a twenty-a-day habit can continue to smoke the remaining seven tabs without forgoing the Dacia.

However, a spokesperson for Dacia UK pointed out, 'If you give up the other seven as well, you could specify some nice extras, like a radio. It's a win-win.' In fact, over three years the optional [*sic*] radio works out at a third of a gasper per day, meaning the Sandero 1.0 SCe cannot mathematically function as a structured programme for giving up addiction to nicotine for anyone smoking more than 13.33₁ fags a day

Meanwhile, drinking enthusiasts might like to consider giving up 1.85675676 pints of beer per day in my local puborama in return for being seen in a brand-new, though radioless, car. It's possible to mangle this nonsense endlessly. For example, giving up one sugar in a cup of tea or coffee would allow anyone drinking five cups a day to buy a base-level

Sandero, outright, for cash, after only 29 years, four months and 24 days (not including radio).

I'm sure you could come up with something equally facile but, as in all exams, I want to see your working out.

Reviewed: noise

There's a new poster ad for a Honda at the end of the road. It says: 'Type R. Hear it roar.' But for how much longer?

As we have discussed on here before, part of the pleasure in driving cars stems from the inadequacies of the internal combustion engine. That we have to change gears, manage revs, avoid bogging the thing down coming out of a tight corner – this sort of thing makes for involvement. There is a deep satisfaction in merely operating the thing.

There's also the sound. There's a glorious bit between 7500 and 9000rpm in my Fezza, where I don't go very often because it's something to be saved up, like your favourite choc in the Christmas assortment tin. Make do with the boring ones in the green foil for a bit, but then treat yourself to the orangey soft centre and enjoy it all the more because you've been denied.

There's a nice bit in my 911, too, when I load the engine up at low revs. It truly does rumble, and I hear it as much with my pelvis as I do with my ears. The Alfa V6 I once had made a lovely burble in the midrange and sounded like a West Country farmer talking about the weather. These are interesting sounds and, in fact, they're part of the feedback at the machine interface.

Most of the time, though, it's just a racket. Most cars sound pretty banal, and many diesel commercials sound downright horrible. Yes, if you're lucky, your car might reward you as you drive with a little sonic titillation once in a while, like my 458 does. But if you're having a nice picnic or trying to bag some zeds, it is, once again, an annoying noise.

I can imagine a time, not far off, when the noise of cars becomes socially unacceptable. It will be viewed in the same light as randomly shouting at people. Many aspects of the car have already been the subject of reform: its sharp edges, its smell, its emissions, its reusability. Next it will be the noise it makes.

I thought I should warn you.

Ferrari safety car

I've often felt that having all-wheel drive in a road car is a bit like having an airbag. It's nice to know it's there if you're caught unawares, but if you're driving at the point where the odd bit of power delivery to the front wheels is going to save you, then you should probably back off a bit. You shouldn't actively exploit it. Otherwise it's a bit like braking very late as you approach the back of a traffic jam, in the certain knowledge that the steering wheel will explode safely in your face if you cock it up.

So I've never quite seen the point of the Ferrari GTC4 Lusso, because you're paying a hefty premium for a frankly incomprehensible AWD system involving two slipping clutches on the front wheels and a computerised brain probably a million times more powerful than the one that took the Apollo astronauts to the moon, etc., etc.

Now I don't have to see the point, because in V8 and turbocharged 'T' form, the Ferrari GTC4 LussoT (*geddit?*) is simply rear-drive. As usual, Ferrari is claiming this is not just a cheaper, less sophisticated two-wheel-drive version of the V12 car, even though it is cheaper, less sophisticated and two-wheel drive. It's a different sort of concept. Obvs.

Or, thinking about it a different way, bollocks. Or is it? I thought so, until I looked more closely at the work of the cavallino rampante departamente marketiano. The car is intended for people who drive 'mostly in high to medium-grip conditions'. And that's me.

I realise that I've been waiting all my life for this. I especially hate slippery roads, and would love to buy a car emphatically unsuited to them, if only such a thing existed. It does now, and top marks to Ferrari for recognising that grip is an issue and that cars should be designed to deal with it.

Off I went then, in the 610bhp twin-turbo

front-engined rear-drive Ferrari high-performance estate that Princess Anne would have owned had it been invented when she had her Reliant Scimitar, around the back roads of lovely Tuscany. The whole area was riddled with high to medium grip in a way I'd never noticed before.

I didn't skid at all. Not at the front, not at the back. Not once. It works.

The weight is over

I'm possibly being a bit thick here, but I'm always amazed there's still a minimum weight regulation for Formula 1 cars.

If we take the (often erroneous) view that F1 should be a crucible for new automotive technology, where innovation that will benefit us all is forged in the white heat, etc., etc.,[3] then it would make sense to have no rules at all, except perhaps one limiting the overall energy consumption.

But I accept that this isn't blue-sky R&D; it's a spectator sport, and a business.

---

[3] In case any pedants are reading, I know that crucibles are for smelting, not forging. Bugger off.

But even so, a minimum weight? This is one area where racing technology and the brains behind it all really could benefit you and me. Weight is a pertinent issue at present. Hybrid and electric cars are at a weight disadvantage because extra motors and big batteries are heavy. So weight saving elsewhere is especially important. A bit of help from the big boys wouldn't go amiss, surely?

Even if we put that aside, weight is still something that a racing car designer would want to reduce. It's not only that weight hampers acceleration. The problem of excessive weight (or, more properly, mass) is compounded during cornering. Being allowed to shave weight off might lead to an overtake. Imagine that.

So – back to paragraph one. Am I being a bit thick?

Don't be a fashion victim

When I was a boy, my ambitions were lofty: the unqualified love of all women, being a fighter pilot, that sort of thing. Now I'm a man I have put aside childish things. In fact, my only remaining aim in life is to get to the end of it without running over anyone.

I do worry about this. I'd hate to be dribbling in a rocking chair on the back porch thinking that I was off to meet the maker in the knowledge that something I regard as essentially a hobby had cost someone else's life. What's to be done?

Speed limits, cry some. Many are too low to be reasonable – the British motorways, some dual carriageways – and in any case speed is a bit like farting. You have to know when it's inappropriate. Imagining you're a safe driver simply because you stick to some fairly arbitrary number on a dial is a feeble-minded attempt to absolve yourself of real responsibility. Paying proper attention is more important.

On the other hand, I'm beginning to think that 30mph on the high street running through local Hammersmith is terrifyingly fast. The people of Hammersmith like to wander randomly into the road. And why shouldn't they? It's their road and it's my job not to run them over.

The good news is that the survivability of pedestrians has been greatly improved over my motoring lifetime. Brakes and tyres are better, so are headlights, and so are windscreen wipers. Glasses are better and more people are wearing them. Cars have fewer and fewer sharp edges, and have softer bonnets for local drunks to bounce off. It all bodes well for the fulfilment of my life goals. But there's something else.

As I write, it's winter. The sky gleams like mercury; the air itself seems grey. People wear more clothes in winter and stand out less starkly against the drab

January canvas. It's like a Lowry viewed through a sheet of bog roll. More to the point, though, we are in what some analysts would regard as a recessionary colour period. Times are uncertain, and this is reflected in the cars we choose. Look what's trendy: grey, silver and dark blue. Meanwhile, the vogue in clothing is for autumnal hues and earth colours, such as browns and russet.

Combine these and you can see a problem. The car is slightly less visible and so is the person. It might add only a fraction of a second to my response time, but that might be the difference between a Hammersmith native doing a comedy hop and skip in the road and going home with a busted leg. Bright paint and a fashion for floral prints must, perforce, make a difference.

Think about this next time you buy a car, because the case for my bright orange Ferrari is stronger than I thought. I know my shirts are pretty terrible, too, but hey, I'm still alive. Look out of the window when you're driving and look before you cross the road. But remember: Paul Smith could save your life.

Fast cars – not fast

I realise this is going to sound a bit of a first world problem, but it's been troubling me for a bit. My Porsche 911 is no faster than my other half's Fiat Panda. Not in reality.

We have a small hobbity cottage in the sticks, about 95 miles from our real house in modern London. At the end of a typical country weekend of witch burning, we set off home. Sometimes, for boring logistical reasons, we're in separate cars. Bridget (I've changed her name to protect her identity; she's actually called Sarah) is always in her Panda, I can be in virtually anything, but in the following illustration I'm in my 911 C2S.

(For the record, the Panda has 69bhp, a top speed of 102mph and does 0–60mph in around 13 seconds. Porsche: 380bhp, 187mph, 4.7 seconds.)

Our old-fart departure routine runs thus: Bridget sets off, I stay to double-check that the house is locked up properly, then I drive out of the, um, drive, get out to shut the gate and then I'm on my way. This takes around three minutes.

First, there are eight miles of villagey bollocks and people in stocks to go through, and I always do this carefully in case any bears have escaped. But then I arrive at 40 miles of lovely open A-road, much of it dual carriageway, where I can gi'e it a bit of shoe.

I'm always amazed at how far I've gone before I overtake Bridget's Panda.

But overtake I do, with a pip and a cheery wave, and pretty soon I'm joining the motorway, which I'm on for another 45 miles. Now it's one of those smart motorways, with the occasional average speed check, but even so, I'm in a 911. Wahey.

Motorway turns back to dual carriageway, with camera-controlled limits, but it leads to within half a mile of the house and in any case, I'm miles ahead. All that remains is to put the Porker back in the garage, which is just around the corner from our front door, and walk fifty paces to the cold embrace of something from the fridge.

But when I arrive at the house, the Panda is parked outside and Bridget is already pouring a couple of tall ones.

That's the harsh truth of it. The Porsche 911, the paradigm for a fast, comfortable, long-legged sports/touring car, is no faster than an Italian peasant farmer's runabout. And so you know, this same experiment has been conducted as Ferrari 458 versus electric BMW i3. The result is the same.

I could explain what's happening here with some graphs and arithmetic, but nothing this side of an Oasis lyric is more meaningless. So-called 'fast cars' simply aren't fast. If your daily commute is 100 miles each way on a derestricted German autobahn, maybe there would be a difference; otherwise, every car you can see out of your window right now goes at exactly the same speed.

Fast cars 'still not fast'

I knew when I wrote that previous article that a lot of you would respond with, 'Yeah, but that's because you're Captain Slow lol crappy smiley face with tears to show I'm not really funneh.' So here's version two.

This time, we shared the house-locking duties. I remained only for the gate closing, an activity of such deep significance in this ongoing experiment that it's become known as 'Gategate'.

This time, though, we took the low route. Instead of turning north and enduring all the Middle Ages before the big dual carriageway, we turned south, which takes us straight to a nice A-road. Sal (she's still called Sarah in real life) was but a minute ahead.

She was also still in the Panda, with the usual plant pots. I was in the new Alpine ('Alpeen') A110. It has 248bhp, weighs the square root of diddly and is the greatest thing to come out of France since the Mouli cheese grater.

There are some single-file roadworks on this stretch, controlled by lights, and I arrived at them on a red. It's a long red. I treated the lights as a drag-strip Christmas tree and I think the bloke waiting at the other end was alarmed at the speed with which I dispatched the bollarded chicane.

I caught up with her outdoors within a couple of miles. And sat behind her through another succession of villages. I really wish people wouldn't live in the countryside. It's for driving through and looking at.

But then a straight bit. I banged it down a couple of cogs and flew away quicker than the yellow bird up high in banana trec. Now I arrived at Salisbury, which adds a frisson of excitement to the contest through the risk of being poisoned.

I couldn't help noticing, as I slowed for various roundabouts and what have you, that although the rear-view mirror of the Alpine is comically small and the view quite restricted, it was big enough to reveal the grinning visage of the woman I love and who loves me as she continually pulled up behind.

But, after a bit more urban sprawl and tortuous back road, it was time to rejoin the fast dual carriageway of the original route. I'm ahead, but it's my job (as IC internet, light bulbs and groceries) to stop at the supermarket with petrol pumps attached and buy ingredients for supper.

I went round the shelves like a ram raider and was back in the Alpine in under three minutes. Then I was back on the slip road to the motorway and you know how the route goes from then on.

A few things to bear in mind. Sal will never go above 70mph on a motorway or dual carriageway. I will. We both stick rigorously to urban speed limits, because we expect other people to do the same through our village. We both used the same route, as usual.

More importantly, however, I didn't have to put the car in the garage, because it's not mine and I was using it early the next day anyway. Ha! So this time I aimed for our little side road with the intention of parking right outside the front door.

At that moment the phone rang. It was Sal. How far off was I, and did I want a glass of the Riesling?

Look, the Alpine A110 is genuinely fast. It is also an adorable car. It will enrich your life, certainly, but it won't save any of it.

The style counsel

What is it that makes old Ferraris so valuable? Not, I would venture, the way they drive.

Since all old Ferraris are just old cars, and old cars are pretty terrible compared with their modern equivalents, no person who otherwise qualified for a shotgun licence would want one for the purposes of driving. Agreed, an old Ferrari is more exciting than an equally old mainstream Ford saloon, but either way you'd rather drive a current Focus. If you've got any sense.[4]

So if we put aside actual driving, what are we left with? Rarity, certainly, but the Citroën Pluriel is

---

[4] I'm not suggesting that you should have any sense. I don't have much. That's why we're interested in cars. Read on.

mercifully rare and no one is going to sleep and dreaming of finding one in a barn. There's the reassurance of race breeding, which definitely counts for something, but again, the Subaru Impreza has a magnificent competition pedigree and an old one can still be yours for the price of a slap-up fish supper.

It's the styling. Because technology dates, eventually to the point of uselessness, the aesthetic is triumphant. That's immediately true of high art, which has no utility, and it's ultimately true of things like cars, which have a purpose to start with but eventually exist solely as part of the story of design, since driving them is awful (see above).

Hang on, I hear you cry as one from the collective lavatory seat of the globe, other cars have fantastic styling as well. They do, but Ferrari's master stroke is this: Ferrari has only ever built contemporary cars.

If you look at the history of Ferrari design, you will struggle to identify any obvious and recurring 'design cues' or stylistic leitmotif in the shapes, beyond the badge. A Ferrari is always of its time: a Testarossa (the *Wolf of Wall Street* one) is quintessentially 1980s, the Boxer was obviously of the 1970s and the 250 GT SWB the very early 1960s. Being of its time, a Ferrari, in time, naturally assumes the right position in this thing we call design history. It helps, of course, that Ferraris have been the work of master stylists, but even so. They seem to me always to have seized the moment, looks-wise.

There is a lesson here, because many other marques haven't had the courage to do this. Two examples – but there are many more – are Alfa Romeo and Aston Martin. Both of these makers have produced radically modern-looking cars in the past, such as the Lagonda in the case of Aston and the Montreal from Alfa. Aston also produced the bulldog concept car, and Alfa has probably produced more outrageous show cars than any other maker.

More recently, though, Astons and Alfas have been tainted with design nostalgia, which is often passed off as 'heritage' but is really a form of timidity. Aston is still headbanging a grille that is supposed to hark back to the DB grilles of the *Goldfinger* era, and Alfas often look good in profile only to be spoiled by front and rear lights that seem to be designed to invoke some earlier age. It's comforting, doubtless, but also a bit square.

If you take this sort of thing to its natural conclusion, you arrive at the pastiche cars: the Fiat 500, the

Mini, the Dodge Challenger. No one in the future is going to remember a car that looks a bit like (but usually not as good as) one that went forty or fifty years before, which means the car is not fulfilling part of its essential work as a thing that people look at every day. Car designers must be modern, or there won't be any interesting history in the future.

It's not about a style language. It's about the language of style. Very different.

Ferraris are cheap to run, says Ferrari

In a surprising diktat directed at Britain's motoring writers, Ferrari's UK office has warned that buying and owning a new Ferrari doesn't really cost anything.

On the eve of the launch of the new Portofino, Ferrari instructed its guests not to write that the Ferrari will cost a lot to run, 'because it's not true'. Since all new Ferraris come with a seven-year servicing package, improved fuel economy and high residual values, 'running a Ferrari is not significantly more than your average family saloon'.

James May said, 'At first I thought this was a load of prancing horse's arse, but then I thought about it a bit harder. My 458 is still worth as much as I paid for it, the servicing costs nothing, and because I'm too scared to drive it the fuel economy is unbelievable. It's actually a free car. I'm absolutely delighted.'

Phil Forecourt, the chairman of Dacia's UK importer, said, 'We were hoping Ferrari wouldn't bring this up. But it's absolutely true. Why buy a Sandero? It's like throwing thousands of pounds down the drain. Buy this 600 horsepower convertible instead. Save your money.'

We rang Ferrari's UK head office for a comment, and a man said, 'That Angelina Jolie definitely fancies you. You're in there, fat man.'

Ferrari 488 Pista – no sale

I probably shouldn't reveal this, because it's a bit like betraying the Magic Circle. Shortly before that secret party where the 488 Pista was revealed to a select audience (and then posted on DriveTribe and Twitter), I received a phone call.

It was my dealer. Ferrari dealer, I mean, but as we're talking about a drug of sorts, it amounts to the same as the thing you just thought.

Did I want one? As a 458 Speciale owner, I had first dibs, but I had to decide by Monday. It was Saturday.

I admit I struggled a bit with this one. The Pista looks fantastic. When I first saw the pictures I had to curl up in a corner and gibber for a bit. It's the most powerful V8 Ferrari to date, and the race-car tech transfer is apparently the most authentic it's ever been.

And, to be brutally mercenary about it, I could probably sell my Speciale for more than the Pista would cost. So it's a new Fezza and change for a slap-up fish supper, as they say in *Viz* comic.

But I couldn't do it. I've owned many cars, but the Speciale is more 'mine' than any other I've had. Ferrari agreed to make one more, just for me, after the order books had closed. I spent a whole day in Italy, in the Ferrari Atelier studio, with the lovely Maria, selecting every last detail of it. I was intending to have a dark blue one but ended up with an orange one, with gold wheels, and stripes. It's the most epic thing I've ever had. It's even better than the Airfix 1/24th scale Supermarine Spitfire.

How could I part with it, the last naturally aspirated V8 Ferrari in history? How could I live knowing that some other peasant was farting in my car?

Someone can have it when I'm dead.

Posh 600hp roadster
'A right laugh'

Hot on the heels of claims that the new Ferrari Portofino is virtually free to own comes further news that it's actually pretty good.

The Portofino is successor to the California, and is bigger all round, more powerful and better looking. Ferrari's 'entry-level' hard-top convertible is now named after a stylish Italian fishing village and resort with an underwater statue of Jesus, instead of an inhabited desert full of people eating hamburgers bigger than their own heads.

With a 0–60mph time of under 3.5 seconds and a top speed nudging 200mph, the Portofino goes 'like an absolute bastard', says DriveTribe's James May. 'It's a right laugh.'

'I've been driving around in it for hours,' he says. 'It's everything you want in a tasteful open car, with the added benefit of being a Ferrari. It's better than working in a bank, that's for sure.'

Costing just £166,180, the Portofino represents a low-cost portal to Ferrari ownership for people who might be feeling the pinch a bit. 'When you look at it like that, it's a bit of a bobby bargain,' says May. 'I know people who have spent that much on a house.'

May continues: 'It would be churlish to try to pick fault with it. It even smells nice. It farts pleasingly at each upshift and the gears change with a satisfying little kick in the coccyx. You come up behind an old Fiat Stilo – blam! It's gone. A mid-sized Citroën – blam! blam! That's gone, too. It really is incredible how useful 600 horsepower is when everyone else only has around 150.'

Asked to sum up his day at the wheel of the new Portofino, May said, 'There are many things wrong with the world at the moment, of course. But this isn't one of them.'

The suspension of disbelief

I woke up the other day and realised I'd spent a goodly part of the last twenty years of my life banging on about the ride in cars. I could have spent the time learning to play the violin, or having a nice lie down.

No one else gives a toss, at least not in the way I do. Nothing else can explain why the vast majority of cars have a middling to truly rotten ride. And this is not just an old fart 'these modern cars are rubbish' rant. It's been the same throughout history, and I've now been around for a fair bit of that.

Ride: it's a complex subject and means different things to different people and, indeed, cars. The new Civic Type R delighted me, because the rock-hard ride

of the old one had given way to a hint of initial supple-
ness that I can only compare with putting one of those
gel liners in a pair of top-shelf training shoes. The
deadly serious sporting intent is still there, but there's
a touch of mercy.

Some Bentley Continentals have also done this well,
a sort of sophisticated firmness.

But as for cars with what I'd call 'a really lovely ride';
well, they are few and far between. They stick in my
mind, like the memory of a boil I had on my leg aged
six, they're that rare. The Jag XJ12 saloon was one, but
that was back in the black and white of my twenties.
The Rover 75, God rest its bones, had a fabulous ride,
because its designers thought the Nürburgring was
something that happened during the rise of fascism.
The Rolls-Royce Ghost has a tremendous ride, but so
it should. How else is a pissed aristocratic driver
supposed to get any sleep?

Now I'd like to move on to this new Audi A8. I've
long had an uneasy relationship with Audis. I often
think they're very good, and they're always beautifully
made, but I find them a bit businesslike. And a lot of
them ride like a handcart that's taking us to hell.

The A8 – my test car was the long wheelbase version – commends itself in the usual ways. It looks pretty good, it's meticulously manufactured, as ever, and it's especially tasteful on the inside. The surface finishes and touchscreen interfaces are all a joy to behold and use.

But the ride: holy crap, it's fantastic. This feels like the hover car I was promised in 1970s sci-fi comics. As I drove by a deliberately circuitous back-road route from our office to the *Grand Tour* tent, I felt the cares of the years caressed out of me by the butt-fondle of properly set-up suspension. It's reason enough to buy this car, because everything else about it is an Audi and therefore nothing to worry about.

Did you buy an S-class or 7-series recently? Please check the returns policy.

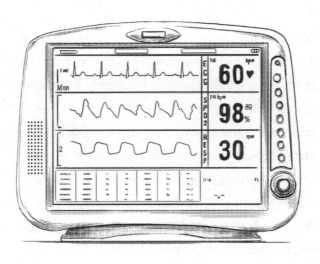

Lose pounds quickly

Back in the very early days of cars, they were 'series produced' but not yet truly mass produced; that is, each was a faithful copy of an original, but not yet built with interchangeable parts made to strict tolerances.

So the people assembling the cars were 'fitters', meaning they had to massage the parts to make them go together – ease out a hole, scrape a bearing surface away slightly and so on. With time and experience, they learned to achieve assembly removing less and less material, which led to something called 'dimensional creep'. The finished cars grew minutely larger.

Cars have been getting bigger ever since. We all know that a new VW Polo is bigger than the original

Golf, and that a so-called Mini has the same wheelbase as the first Range Rover. Is there a car that became smaller? I don't think so.

A lot of people imagine that the rash of short cars we've seen over the last decade – starting, famously, with the Smart ForTwo – will ease congestion, but I'm not so sure. It's great for parallel parking, but not traffic jams. The length of the road is not the issue. It's the width.

It's therefore the width of cars that counts, and my concern is not with congestion, but fun. Cars are getting wider as well as longer and taller. Meanwhile, the sort of road where a supercar would be a right laugh hasn't really evolved that much. I'm talking about winding back roads in England, Italy, France. They've been the same width since the Middle Ages.

The Ferrari GTC4 Lusso I drove last week is a tremendous car, but it would be even more tremendous if I could've punted it with vigour down a B road. I couldn't, not with complete confidence, because it was often more than half a road wide, and Antonio could be coming the other way in his van.

Now I have a 308 as well, I realise how much bigger

the 458 is. It's 217mm wider, which isn't a lot if you're buying a house but a hell of a lot when you're driving a car. Look at 217mm on your ruler. You get that much extra clearance on one side, in effect, because the other side of the car is at the edge of the road.

Extra power begets fatter wheels, which means more bodywork and more weight, and needs a beefier gearbox, and so it goes on. I want Ferrari to make something mid-engined but not much bigger than an MX-5; with a fizzy 2.5-litre turbo V8 of 375hp and weighing not more than a tonne. Fastest car in the real world, probably.

I'm avoiding saying 'Dino', because that's what everyone always says. But you know what I mean.

Hammond bins it

What I saw, as I passed the finish line, was a car, on its roof, way down the steep slope on the grass below. It was burning ever more furiously.

What was it? It was impossible to equate that blazing and charred heap with the exquisite, pearl-white electrical delicacy that had sat in front of my Honda, at the start line, less than two minutes ago.

But I knew, in the blossoming, white-hot ball of pure, sickening horror forming in my heart, that it must be Hammond's Rimac.

The next thing I registered, as I stopped and scrambled from the car, was a pair of marshals dragging a limp body by the wrists, away from the wreck and down to a gravel path at the bottom of the hill. And I knew that must be Richard Hammond.

I cannot remember experiencing such a debilitating sense of shock and pure incomprehension as this.

There we were, at the start line of this good-humoured family motor sport event, swapping insults with each other and our director over our radios, awaiting our turns for a run up the hill.

Hammond was first and disappeared like some weird antimatter-powered javelin, almost silently. Twenty seconds later I was waved away to be met, three turns before the end, with a flurry of yellow flags and then a world unutterably changed. Hammond was dead.

However, the window of opportunity for believing that Hammond was dead was quite brief. I happened to have driven through the middle of it.

Maybe fifteen seconds earlier, and I would have seen a dazed but intact Hammond extracting himself from his lunched but not yet burning car.

About a minute after I went into a blue funk, one of our sound men ran over to tell me that he still had 'ears' on Hammond's microphone, and that he was talking perfect sense to the paramedics.

I happened to arrive as the marshals pulled him hurriedly away from the newly burning car because they thought it might explode. But what I saw was the remains of Hammond being hauled from the burning wreckage, like some hideous vintage film clip from Formula 1.

It's important to see the whole scenario and not rely on a snapshot. I thought he'd bought the farm, but he'd actually broken a bone in his knee and needed a small pin putting in it; in Switzerland, the world centre of skiing injuries and doing things properly.

Far from being dead, he even came home slightly improved over the Brummie original.

Man buys car

Every now and then, I try to buy Richard Hammond's E-type Jag. It's not for sale and I don't really want it anyway. I just like winding him up by making insultingly low offers and then trying to browbeat him into selling it to me.

Once or twice I think I've come close – through a combination of subterfuge, chicanery and man maths – to making him give it up. But not quite. Still, it's a good game on a long aeroplane flight, or similar.

Trouble is, this has been going on for a long time, and it's now become a matter of personal honour to succeed in buying Hammond's E-type against his will.

Even though I don't really want it. And now I have a new plan.

A few years back, I bought a bike from Hammond, and paid him using online banking. So he's in there as a past payee. So what I thought I'd do, without telling him, is transfer the value of the E-type (about £20k) to his account, and in the box where you write the details for the payee's statement, put 'Payment in full for E-type Jag'. Then I'd do nothing for a year.

Hammond won't notice this. I happen to know that his wife checks the bank statements, and she won't be at all surprised to see another transaction relating to one of those numerous leaky heaps living in his garage. Happens all the time.

After a year, I'll take him to the small claims court, pointing out that I paid for the car – and here's the bank statement to prove it – but that he's never handed it over. Then it will be mine.

Look out for me, in it, in 2018.

Hamster job
prospects update

It's probably not that great being Richard Hammond post his Swiss hill climb get-off. I doubt it was ever that brilliant, to be honest, but now he has to lie there, half legless, absorbing the full weight of his coevals' wit and humour, totally defenceless.

It's hard not to join in. When I was with him in the hospital, straight after the binning, a nurse came in and said she'd come to 'clean him up'. I had to dive in and explain that the beard and 'tache combo are supposed to be there, and to leave them.

More to the point, there's been some speculation as to Hammond's short-term future as a man who makes a living driving around in cars and talking about them, in a slightly chirpy voice. Because, for now, he only has one leg.

Autonomous cars, suggest some. Motability cars for the disabled, say others. And these are worthy suggestions, but hang on. It's his left leg.

Now, when I started in this business, busting the knee of your left leg would have condemned you to months of misery on the mid-range diesel automatic executive saloon giant test, but it's not like that any more. I think it's fair to say that the most interesting and exciting cars currently being made are all one-leg, two-arm propositions. Anything electric and futuristic, any AMG Merc, all the interesting 911s. I'm beginning to think that using your left leg to drive is a bit cubic.

And all supercars. They all have two pedals and paddles. Unless Hammond really is thinking of reviewing an arse-kicking contest, I can't see that he needs his left leg at all for work.

In fact, I'm beginning to wonder if he's pulled a bit of a blinder. I can see a near future where we're divvying up cars to drive on the show, and Hammond will always end up in the McLaren or the Lambo because of the leg issue, and I'll have the base-spec saloon because I can still work the forgotten pedal on the left. I am reminded of my brother always getting more roast turkey at Christmas, because he claimed he didn't like the sprouts or parsnips. I got extra veg.

Seriously, he's pretty much guaranteed a good time in great cars. Take my beloved bright orange Ferrari. He'll have no problem in that. He can pop it in wet mode and fully automatic and trundle around town like a midwife in an old CVT Volvo. But when he gets to those lovely sweeping roads near his house, he can twist the Manettino switch to 'sport' or even 'race', switch out the auto changes and let his fingers do the important work; mining the glorious and sonorous reaches of the last naturally aspirated Ferrari V8's upper rev range as he howls towards the uphill right-left flick, brakes, drops two or three cogs with nothing more than a dismissive hand gesture and then plants the pedal and lunges . . .

Um, on second thoughts . . .

Gentlemen, hide your engines

A lot of people on here view the internal combustion engine in the way some Americans view the right to bear arms. It's not just necessary, it's a principle, and a zealously defended one.

I'm with you all, up to a point. We love our cars, but what we love most about them is that convoluted enclosure of flailing metal that gives the impression of personality, because the internal combustion engine is crammed with engaging flaws, as are we.

And so we prostrate ourselves before the piston god, swearing allegiance for ever, and electricity is the infidel. But for how much longer?

As the poet Philip Larkin said, 'I thought it would

last my time,' but now I'm not so sure. The way things are going, there's a good chance that, within a decade, your V8 twin turbo supercar engine is going to be about as welcome as a double-ended dipstick. Then what are we going to do? Strimmers and lawnmowers don't quite hack it.

May I suggest a motorcycle? For a start, there is huge variety in bike engines: singles, parallel twins, flat twins, V-twins with pushrods that cure backache, V-twins with Desmo valves that thrash your brain, triples, fours, a few sixes, engines in line with the frame and across it – it goes on and on. Because of the way a motorcycle is connected to its user, they all offer top quality holy communion and introduce you to endless new ways for putting a little tingle in your coccyx.

More to the point, nobody takes any notice of bikes. Most people don't know what they are. Legislators largely ignore them, road safety evangelists ignore them, environmental activists ignore them; there are so few motorcycles compared with cars, vans and trucks that they are statistically irrelevant, so no one gives a toss. Good news! Keep a motorcycle tucked away somewhere and you will still be able to worship regularly, even though the institution will seem to have faded away.

'Through Him all things were made; without Him nothing was made that has been made,' (John 1:3). So that must include my Honda CBR600RR. Cheers, guy in the sky with the beard by ZZ Top, because I still think it's the fizzingest thing I've ever owned. It's not an expensive toy, not compared with even a Golf GTI, let alone anything with the engine in the middle. It has but an in-line four, like a Ford Cortina, but in reality it's properly race-bred, because the process of optimising its valve gear and piston/cylinder dimensions began with Soichiro Honda on the Isle of Man, long before I existed.

And when you ride it, the engine seems to be not underneath the fairing but buried somewhere deep in your bowels. It sparkles everywhere and can be wrung out to 15,000rpm (if you have a desperate urge to express your support for the nation's health service). It's intoxicating and why would you not want that?

Come to church, everyone. You will be blessed.

See that cow?
That'll do 180

Years ago, I met the owner of some 1960s American coupé or other who claimed that his car developed 850 horsepower. Never mind that the pistons seemed to slap like a fishmonger's slab or that all he'd really done was fit some different carbs and polished the air filter casing. It was 850 horses, and that was a fact.

Now I've heard about someone who's turbo-charged a V8 pick-up and got his mate to reprogram the ECU with his iPhone, and that develops 1500 horsepower.

Look, the unit of horsepower (hp) was quantified by James Watt, he of steam engine fame, so that mine owners could get an idea of how many pump-driving pit ponies one of Watt's beam engines would replace. One horsepower would lift 33,000lb one foot in one minute. This is sometimes referred to as 'Imperial horsepower'.

The 'brake horsepower' (bhp) we talk about in car engines is a related unit, differing mainly in that it is calculated by applying a resistance to the rotating crankshaft (the 'brake' bit) to make the engine run at a given speed, and then calculating power from the amount of 'braking' required (this is a massive simplification).

But we are now ready for a new unit, hpma, or horse power my arse. That pick-up, I'm fairly confident, develops 1500hpma. Meanwhile, the credible original Bugatti Veyron gives 1000bhp. Doesn't sound as impressive, but it's a different unit.

Interestingly, a while back I met a man at a car festival with a trailer-mounted dynamometer who would happily test people's claims. I can't remember what he called his business, to be honest.

But I can remember that, off the record, he referred to it as 'the lie detector'.

The Mixtures were full of shit

The bicycle is living in troubled times. Cycling, once merely a means of transport for the poor and those too small to operate cars safely, is now an instrument of urban revolution, a statement, a political badge of allegiance. Once, people were described as 'a card-carrying (insert political or social persuasion)', but now they ride bicycles.

But, really, this is all twaddle. There is an outspoken bicycle lobby, just as there's one for cars, trains, line dancing and Belgium, but to most of us a bike is simply a useful ingredient of the personal transport minestrone, and quite good fun. Riding a bicycle feels good.

I like a bicycle and I differ from my colleagues on

this one. I haven't been without a bicycle since I was three years old, and have done many thousands of miles on them. So when some berk with polystyrene bananas on his head starts lecturing me about the importance of cycling – as if the thing has just been invented and only he's heard of it – I want to tell them how I was prised from mine outside the Dalwhinnie distillery in Scotland, frozen in the attitude of a cyclist, by a kindly old Scottish lady who filled me with whisky and hot chocolate and then booted me back out into the rain to complete the remaining thirty miles to Aviemore.

Still, the bicycle is one of the most important inventions in history. It's reckoned to be twenty times as efficient as walking, but is still a form of pedestrianism. It's leg-powered, and essentially free. It's also unregulated, slightly anarchic and possibly plays an important role in the model for utopia.

Meanwhile, we should probably learn to ride them properly. I've been doing a fair bit of recreational cycling lately, simply because I'm feeling old and I've got a bad back. It's knackering but, after all this time, not difficult.

Sometime around the age of three and a bit, my dad whipped the stabilisers off my Raleigh Mayflower,[5] gave me a short shove and off I went. I could ride a bike and I've been able to do it ever since, because it's a bit like riding a bike.

But then fifty years later, during a sleepless night and when all the usual internet distractions had been exhausted, I started reading learned articles about cycling. And it turns out I've been doing it wrong. Here's one I especially liked: http://www.bicycling.com/training/fitness/perfect-pedal-stroke.

Now don't get bogged down in the stuff about heart rates. Look at the diagram on how to work the pedals. That bit about the power stroke part of the . . . cycle.

I tried this, on one of my regular evening rides by the riverside. Bugger me if the bike didn't suddenly set off like I'd lit a RATO unit strapped to my seat stem. I was gasping slightly less than usual, but the bike was going a good 20 per cent faster. Houses, ducks and other cyclists flashed past in reverse and I was at the pub before I knew what had happened.

---

[5] Imagine how pleased I was to own a bike with my name in it.

Then I started watching other people on bikes. The lycra brigade do it right, of course, but most cyclists are only people riding bikes. And they're a bit hopeless. Half of them ride with their feet and knees all over the place like a cartoon midwife. They look ridiculous.

And, while I'm at it, use the gears properly as well. I see some riders pulling away from rest in 24th and barely able to balance, and others whose legs are going round so fast their kneecaps are going to boil away. Change gear. The power band of a bicycle (i.e. the rider) is very narrow, so, as with a big truck, you need lots of gears and you need to change between them constantly.

And that means whatever gear change system your bike has must work properly, but few of them do, because no one ever does any bicycle maintenance. How have we arrived at this? How has the technical literacy of our society evolved to the point where this global and interactive digital edifice can exist, but no one can make the few simple adjustments necessary to make a bicycle derailleur shift correctly? With a handful of pressed-steel spanners, a couple of screwdrivers and a tube of grease, you can make any bicycle work beautifully.

Your bicycle is a great liberator, first base in a lust for mobility that leads all the way to the Lamborghini Aventador. If you're going to do it, do it properly. You're wasting your breath.

I hate drifting

'Everybody likes a good bit of drifting,' said Richard Hammond, once, but he's wrong. I'm part of everybody and I hate it.

I accept that drifting takes a good deal of skill. So does playing the hurdy-gurdy, but that's no excuse for doing it. Like the hurdy-gurdy recital, drifting makes a godawful racket but also a terrible smell, so as a form of entertainment it ranks alongside someone playing the hurdy-gurdy while simultaneously cooking a packet of condoms on a barbecue.

For some reason, no car-themed event is now considered complete unless someone is making a deliberate balls-up of a simple corner; viz. the London

Motor Show a couple of weeks ago. This 'featured' a continuous display of indoor drifting.

So there I was, trying to talk to an interesting bloke about the new TVR, but I couldn't really hear what he was saying because of the ritual rubber sacrifice taking place at one side of the arena. And when I got home my shirt smelled like a burnt-out slot car. It's antisocial.

What really alarms me is that drifting seems to have been invented by the Japanese. I'm a big fan of Japan, having spent quite a bit of time there. Everything is exquisite: the fuel-station etiquette, the small rituals, the view of Mount Fuji in the morning mist, even the way they wrap and present a simple boiled sweet. It's all wonderful.

Some Japanese enthusiasms can seem a little eccentric. On one visit, I seemed to have arrived in the middle of a craze for dressing up as Elvis Presley, which is a difficult look to pull off if you're five-foot six, of slight build, Japanese, and culturally averse to the idea of a cheeseburger. On another trip I found myself in the Museum of the Vulva, which was a garden shrine dedicated to naturally occurring objects that happened to resemble, vaguely, the silken purse. But because it was Japanese, it was excruciatingly tasteful.

But now it turns out they invented drifting, which obfuscates all their other achievements with a grey/blue fug. And here we are in the West being worried about North Korea.

What is it that's so offensive about drifting? I think it's because drifting is like a form of performance mooning. The car approaches the bend, flashes its arse at the baying crowd, and farts.

It's disgusting.

Reviewed: flatulence

I've never admitted to this before, but many years ago, when I was a starving freelance writer living in a freezing garret, I wrote the sales brochure for the then-new Suzuki Liana.

'Liana' was a name that baffled many people. It was meant to stand for Life In A New Age, which seemed like a bit of a stretch if you actually drove one. There was never really a sense of moving into a new and utopian age of man, more that you were driving around in a small, clunky car with a face like a freshly kicked arse. Suzuki Flafka would have been quite a good name, in fact.

'Ignis' sounds like another silly acronym. It's Great Now In Suzuki, or something. In fact it's derived from *ignis fatuus*, the scientific name for a will-o'-the-wisp, or friar's lantern. This is the ghostly light seen over marshland, caused by the release of trapped gases, especially methane. So there you go. It's the Suzuki Fart.

All Suzukis have terrible interior door trim and smell funny, not just the Fart. But apart from that, it's really rather good.

This one is the range-topping SZ5 SHVS, SHVS standing for Shit Happens Vehicle System. Not really, it's Smart Hybrid Vehicle (by) Suzuki. The 'mild' hybrid system (their word; it's not an aggressive hybrid that knocks your pint over and then kicks your head in) comprises a simple starter/generator and an AA battery under the passenger seat. The whole lot weighs only 6.2kg, and the whole car is commendably light at 920kg. If you choose the basic front-wheel-drive version, it's just 855kg. Bashin'.

This is not a Prius. The hybrid stuff is only something that's there. You can't drive it on pure electric power, it just goes, like a car. Even the simple dash graphic showing how electrical energy is flowing looks as though it was drawn by the people who did BBC Ceefax in the 1980s.

Blah blah blah. It's a car and it might work quite well off road, like the Jimny did, because it's so light and can skip around like a randy goat. It has a hill descent system. I haven't tried any of this because deliberately driving off road is like owning a kitchen and then deliberately having a barbecue.

What I have done is drive around in the Fart as if it were my car, and it's really good. The engine (1.2 litres) is quite sweet, the hybrid system is seemingly effective but ignorable, it rides well, it's well equipped, it looks amusing and it comes in wacko colours. It weighs bugger all and costs from just £13,575. It must be made from cheese and full of helium.

Best of all, though, it feels incredibly good-humoured. Farting is still funny, and so is this car.

Internal combustion – a bit of a faff, really

The reason we, as car enthusiasts, love our engines is because they have a great deal of mechanical character. There are sweet spots in the power band, strange vibrations, torquey engines, revvy engines and so on.

But if we take a step back and stop being so sentimental, what we're really talking about is serious flaws in the original idea.

Let's take the relatively simple example of the 1.2 petrol engine in the May household Fiat Panda. The pistons go up and down as fuel is ignited and burned in the cylinders – that's the nub of it. This reciprocating motion is offensive to good engineering thinking because those pistons are flung one way then the other coming to a complete stop twice in each cycle. It's why weightlifting is so exhausting.

This back-and-forth nonsense has to be mechanically converted to rotary motion in the camshaft so the valves can open and close to let fuel in and exhaust out. That's reciprocating motion again. Bugger.

Everything has to be meticulously timed: when the valves open and close, when the spark comes. And these things vary depending on load and engine speed. This is just the beginning.

And let's not forget that all we are really after is a rotating shaft to do the work, and that's all we wanted of the waterwheel, HMS *Victory*'s capstan and windlass, and the treadmill in Pentonville Prison.

There's more. The Panda engine has to idle, even if the car isn't moving. Engine speed is severely limited by all that flying piston and valve stuff, so some sort of gearbox is needed to make it useable over a wide range of road speeds. It then follows that there needs to be some means of disconnecting the engine from the rest of the machinery so you can come to a stop or, in a manual, change gears. And so it goes on.

At the other extreme from the Panda, we might

consider the Bristol Centaurus aero engine. Actually, we might not want to consider it because it's a 53-litre, 18-cylinder, double-row radial with two-stage super-charging and four-port sleeve valves. Best not to think about it, especially if you're sitting right behind one in a Hawker Tempest and depending on it, utterly.

This is why we mustn't dis the electric motor as a means of propelling our day-to-day cars. It makes perfect sense, we've known as much for well over a century, and to deny it is an affront to reason. There are really only two parts to an electric motor – the stationary stator and the rotating, um, rotor. No recip-rocating nonsense. That's why even the basic electric motor in my Hornby Flying Scotsman train set will spin four times as fast as the engine in the Panda. Smooth, quiet, low maintenance: simple as a prospect and in operation.

Don't get me wrong. I love internal combustion. I like to sit and look at the four-pot engine in my Honda CBR600 and marvel at the unimaginable mechanical fury that goes on inside it.

But I'm telling you, it's doomed.

Jacques-in-the-box

If you're from abroad, you may one day come to visit Britain and do a selfie with one of our 'iconic' red phone boxes. You will probably then share it on Insta and perpetuate the image of Britain as a retarded nation of stuckists who can't move on from the era of Bakelite and piss smell. Thanks.

The red phone box is one of the worst things to have happened to us. For though it was superseded by much better public telephonic facilities, we seem to think that losing it will somehow bring the country to ruin. 'It's an important part of our heritage,' someone will say, in the way that my knee jerks when someone hits it with a small rubber hammer. No it isn't. It stinks.

And now Peugeot – who are French and therefore not inclined to help us at the moment – have preserved another one, in London, equipped it with a tablet and 'e-commerce portal', and turned it into what they claim is 'The smallest car dealership in the world'.

Well, it isn't, because I have a much smaller one in my pocket. Using my iPhone, I discover that I can already log on to Peugeot Order Online; in fact, owing to a combination of a hangover and finger-bounce, I almost bought a 2008 SUV by accident.

So let's consider the prospective customer who intends to use the new Russell Square phone box dealership Peugeot portal. This person will walk out of their house, past their desktop computer, their tablet, their smartphone, and possibly their internet-enabled gaming console, and head to a urinary folk throwback to order a car. That is something they could have done sitting on the bog.

Such a person should not be allowed to drive a car.

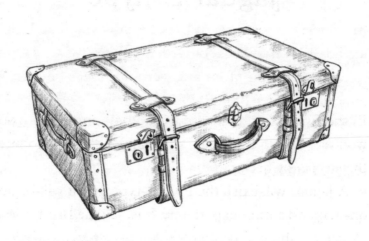

Jaguar E-hype

In the future – in this case from 2040 onwards – you won't be able to buy a Jag. You will only be able to buy the steering wheel.

A Jaguar will exist, the Future-type, but it will be an on-demand sort of experience. It is, say the Brummies, 'A car for the world of autonomous, connected, electric and shared mobility', which gives us the handy acronym ACES. Although they could have gone further, with an autonomous, connected electric, biodegradable, intelligent, still-connected, universally integrated transport solution, or ACEBISCUITS.

I'm not making this up. They are. Sayer – the name they've given to the steering wheel, after the E-type's designer – is 'the world's first intelligent and connected steering wheel', by which they mean connected to the internet. For the first time, it's not necessarily connected to the car. It might be in your bedroom, or that cupboard under the stairs that always has a massive spider in it. It is so much more than a steering wheel, which is a bit last Wednesday. 'It can summon your car, play music, book you a table, and even knows what's in your fridge.'

Why does your steering wheel need to know what's in your fridge? It doesn't. But it can, because it's presumably some kind of tablet, but shaped like a steering wheel.

Jaguar – they're mad, you know – go even further. The steering wheel becomes 'your trusted companion'. This means it will be with you in the trenches. You can take it for walks as an excuse for getting out of the house and away from the other half. You could take it down the pub and talk to it at length about what's in the fridge. It will comfort you in lonely old age, for its love is unqualified. I wish they'd called it Malcolm rather than Sayer.

Here's how it might work in the real world of 2040. You need to be somewhere the next day, at a certain time. You simply tell your Malcolm, and it (he? she?) works out a route and the right departure time, and then when that time arrives, the rest of the Jaguar turns up at your door and off you go, autonomously. It's a bit like an Uber, except it can drive.

Great car, short name

The longest official car name I know harks from Britain in the 1960s. 'Twas then that Rolls-Royce asked its coachbuilding arm to produce a coupé version of its then new Silver Shadow.

Rolls-Royce had absorbed two independent coach-builders, H.J. Mulliner and Park Ward. So the car that would eventually become the Corniche was initially known as the Rolls-Royce Silver Shadow two-door saloon by H.J. Mulliner Park Ward.

Ha! The American website The Daily Drive has a section devoted to cars with long names, but the best the colonials seem to be able to come up with is Oldsmobile Cutlass Supreme Classic Brougham, boasting five words, 10 syllables and 39 characters. But here's Britain batting back with 12 words, 18 syllables and 57 characters (I'm including the hyphens, just to rub it in).

Take that, new-world amateurs. You come in here with your space programme and your refrigerators and your pioneering internet connections between UCLA and Stanford, but you can't give a car a really stupid name, can you? Classic Brougham indeed. Kiss my brogues.

Thing is, no one who owned a Silver Shadow two-door, etc., etc., would ever have called it that. You'd say you had a Rolls-Royce or, if you were really posh, simply a Royce.

In reality, then, the more words you need to establish the credibility of your car, the less credible it is. Maybe. For example, Mini has now launched the new Mini John Cooper Works Clubman (five words, eight syllables, 26 characters). Not a bad name, but if you said only, 'I have a Mini,' that doesn't mark you out as a serious helmsman. You have to add all the works and Cooper stuff to make that clear. A Mini is just a slightly trendy biffabout.

Take the Honda Civic Type R. 'Honda' alone could mean a basic Jazz and often does. 'Civic' doesn't confer much either. You need to say 'Type R' to sound serious about your performance motoring, but by then you might sound a bit desperate as well.

I could go on. I will. Nissan? Could be a Juke, which will get you punched in the face by Richard Hammond. Nissan GT-R is more like it, and if you're with people in the know you could probably get away with just the GT-R bit. Add 'Nismo' or 'Track Edition' and you're trying to make a point. Never good.

Meanwhile, if you have a Lamborghini, you can say as much. 'I have a Lamborghini.' Good, isn't it? It could be a clapped-out Urraco but you still have a Lambo, and you've said enough. Sometimes it's the model name rather than the maker. 'Ferrari' sounds better than admitting to a Mondial, but owning a Corvette is better than having a Chevrolet. Either way, one word is best and if you say 'Vette', you reduce the character count further, admittedly at the expense of sounding like a right turnip.

Good theory, this. I've also realised it works for other things, such as jobs. Teacher? Doctor? Engineer?

I know what you do. But if you're the European Vice-President Market Strategy and Corporate Outreach, I'll worry that you spend too much time polishing your stapler.

First titter of spring not heard in Woking

McLaren Automotive, the Woking-based and famously po-faced purveyor of bespoke British supercars, has today unveiled its first ever joke.

Robin Crane, the bird-brained head of humour at the laugh-proofed underground production facility, told a group of stony-faced reporters, 'Building cutting-edge performance vehicles is no laughing matter! Until now!' Early reactions suggest it still isn't.

The 'feather wrap', applied to a 570GT, is made from the remains of local carbon-fibre crows that have been shot outside the factory for crapping on the grass. It is claimed to reduce turbulence at the boundary layer at high speed and has been created to inject some much-needed bantz into proceedings at the workplace.

'This is our contribution to the tradition of April Fool wit,' says Crane. 'But we have done it on 31st March rather than April 1st, because we wanted to win something.' Rumours suggest next year's joke may be unveiled as early as February.

A public affairs spokesman has vigorously denied claims that this is, in fact, McLaren's second joke, since the touchscreen on the early MP4-12C was 'pretty bloody laughable'.

The car – essentially doomed

I had one of my surreal moments of disbelief the other day when driving the AMG E63 S. This is a 600+ horsepower car that will go from rest to 60mph in 3.4 seconds and on, if unlimited, to 186mph. There are no laws against that. There are rules about how you use it: you're not supposed to drive it on the pavement, and there are speed limits, but as far as I can make out there are no laws governing the performance of cars. You can build a car as powerful and as fast as possible, and it's all perfectly legit.

That is pretty amazing, isn't it? The rules don't allow me to parade a shotgun around the town centre, because of the potential for misuse. But there

I was parading the AMG E63 S, and no one could stop me.

Please don't imagine that I'm about to trot out that tired old argument about the car as an unregulated lethal weapon. I'm actually going to trot out the thought that it's a good thing society still hasn't resolved the debate about the legalisation of drugs, because as long as The Man is worrying about that, he might not notice that some of us are getting whacked off our tits on stuff like AMG, which even sounds a bit Class A.

I've always disliked people who say to me, 'A car is just something to get you from A to B,' because that's a bit like me looking at a Jackson Pollock in a gallery and then saying to the curator, 'A painting is just a splash of colour to relieve the monotony of a plain white wall.' But, when all's said and done, the car is simply a conveyance, like the escalator in an airport, and the E63 S is not really any more effective than a regular dose of Mercedes E. But it is a lot funnier.

Cram in the massive engine and all the other technical accoutrements of high performance and the journey from A to B can be a proper trip. It's like the difference between having a sandwich and being at one of

Laura Nyro's picnics. Why does it feel so good? Do I feel superior? Is it a temporary form of wealth or power? Would I still want to go out and give the AMG E63 S the beans even if I were the only person left on Earth? I think I would. It makes me feel at least as good as James Brown. Briefly.

But that's where it goes slightly wrong for me.

Over the last lifetime or so we have turned the car into a focus for idolatry, a votive object for some form of Satanism, a conduit for exorcising a sense of inadequacy, all sorts of things that are well understood about the relationship between people and cars. We have also turned the act of operating the machine into a mind-altering activity, especially with cars like the E63 S. I'm not talking about the rather esoteric business of deciphering the feedback from a well-composed mid-engined supercar; I'm talking about the cheap thrill of planting your toe and making the view go a bit squiffy. It's allowed. For Pete's sake, don't tell anyone.

But someone I know who's prominent in the world of law – let's say he's a High Court judge – thinks it might not be allowed for that much longer. He says massed car ownership and use may soon be shown to be legally untenable. Then we really will fall foul of The Man and become passengers in pods outside of our control.

I've often thought about this day. I've always argued that driving will eventually become a hobby for those who are interested, because the 'conveyance' bit of the requirement will be met by something else. So circuits and one or two loops of road will be preserved for paying enthusiasts to drive on, rather in the way some canals are still maintained for narrowboat fans. But you won't be able to do it everywhere.

When that time comes, I won't really want the AMG E63 S. It's too much of a conveyance at heart; a saloon car gone bad, rather than a bespoke instrument of driving. I won't want all the seats or the luxury appointments, I'll want only the fizz. The AMG is more of a quick bang, perhaps followed by some paranoia. That said, it's bloody hilarious when it's happening, and while it's still permitted it should be tried.

I think the extinction of the car will be a gradual process, not a catastrophic event. The first to fade away will be these superpower saloons. Then we'll lose SUVs and people carriers, then mainstream hatches and family boxes, then all the small economical runabouts. Finally, we'll be left only with utterly pointless but deliciously indulgent supercars.

I've said it before and I still think I'm right. The future is full of Ferraris.

Reviewed: history

I was building myself up to a big rant about this car. About how the past has gone. That the things we thought precious and the people we held dear are landfill, and all that remains is an impression of how it was, which is inaccurate.

That, of course, those who will not learn from history are doomed to repeat it, or so we are told. Yet here are people who know a great deal about the history of the car but have seen fit to revisit it anyway. Why? For what is history, if not a warning? It's not there to be poked with a pointy stick.

That, in May's Britain, where there will be as few rules as possible, there will nevertheless be a ten-year ban on re-engineering or recreating old cars or pastiches of them, because these activities reveal an inability to move on, in this case to the Kia Picanto GT Line. I quite like that one.

That attempting to relive a past era is like listening to authentic performances of eighteenth-century music. You can get every last detail meticulously period, right down to the catgut used for violin strings, but you can't remove your ears from the present. You cannot hear Bach as Bach's mates did, because you have since heard Beethoven, The Orb and gangsta rap, and you cannot unexperience these things.

But then I calmed down a bit.

I'd better tell you what it is. It's the Mini Remastered by David Brown Automotive, and although it appears to be a 'proper' Mini, most of it is new. It starts, inevitably, with a donor car, but all that survives of that are the engine and gearbox casings and the car's identity plate. Everything else is new.

The body, for example, is a remade heritage job, and even then it's 'deseamed', which was something quite fashionable in the 1970s and 1980s. As an amateur job this was often risky – a bit like deseaming your motorcycle jacket – but we can assume David Brown has done it properly and it won't turn suddenly into a giant Airfix kit when you hit a pothole. I did, it didn't.

In fact, the work is nicely done, if a bit predictable. The engine is bored out to 1300cc (or 1275cc on the more 'basic' version), there are modern lights and electrics, satnav, extra sound deadening, leather everywhere and plenty of hand-made knurled and polished this 'n' that. Prices range from – you are not about to read a typing error – £75,000 to almost £100,000. For a Mini.

It is, says the maker in a rare foray into the twenty-first century, 'Livin' for the City'. These people will be turning up for work without a tie on soon.

It's small, like a Mini, because it is one. Smallness confers benefits, a lesson from history worth learning, and not only when parking. It's so stubby that sometimes you seem to be sitting behind it rather than in it, like that alternative view in a video game.

But history has an ugly side. As in a Mini (because it is one) the ride is bouncy, the steering oddly geared for modern tastes, the engine quite coarse and the racket unbearable. And the number of times I went for fifth or even sixth gear started to make me feel foolish. The past is a foreign country, and there were only four ratios.

Look, it's obviously being touted as a lifestyle accessory. The brochure is full of pictures of people much better looking than me in social situations I cannot aspire to, clutching retro cameras and pouting. Maybe it's just for rich hipsters.

But if you actually like cars, it's a bit confusing. If you're a certified Mini Nazi, you'll want the real thing, seams 'n' all. If you simply want a small car that you can throw into a cul-de-sac with suicidal abandon, you'll want a Suzuki Celerio or a VW Up!

I'll take a VW Up! I think. I'll spend around a quarter of the change on an original Mini Cooper and park it in my sitting room, to remind myself how bad we used to have it.

Autonomy, morality, you

I'd like to narrow the Autonomous Car Morality Debate down a bit, to one facet that I keep hearing when the topic comes up. It's led me to a rather startling conclusion.

Here is the imagined scenario: an autonomous car is travelling along with four people on board. A lorry (or whatever) pulls out in front of it and the car cannot possibly stop in time. Does the car crash into the lorry, killing its four occupants, or does it swerve onto the pavement and kill a single pedestrian who happens to be walking by?

Morally, I think this one is simple. The car should kill its occupants, since they elected to be in it, and the pedestrian is an innocent bystander. 'No!' comes the cry of pretty much everyone else. 'That means four people die instead of only one, and how can that be right?' Because we're talking about morality, which is not to be confused with arithmetic or, worse, the natural and self-preserving instinct of a human driver.

But morality is, indeed, a construct. I don't believe the animals are troubled by it. Certainly my cat isn't. He's a total shit, and if I suddenly became three inches tall he would kill me for his own amusement, even though I rescued him from the cat sanctuary and I've been feeding him for years.

Trouble is, I don't think humans can be perfectly moral, either. It's an ideal, like perfect engine efficiency, but not one that can be achieved. That's OK, because we accept the human fallibility of which we're all guilty, but we don't really accept it in machines. So an autonomous car does, in fact, need a perfect moral compass.

Let's say we could arrive, as humanity, at an agreed universal morality. I think we're pretty close to one, in the temple of our hearts, even if we can't hope to live by it. Now let's say this perfect morality can be turned into an algorithm and installed in the operating system of our robotic car.

This perfect autonomous car can never set off. Because cars themselves are, in fact, immoral.

Musk hints at 'space car'

The head of Tesla, Elon Musk, famous for his free-wheeling thinking on the future of transport, has told DriveTribe that he is working in secret on a type of flying car that could make personal global travel a possibility and demolish the business model of airlines.

'Most flying car concepts are based on airplanes,' says the jazz-fag enthusiast. 'But that's backward thinking. Ours is based on a spaceship.'

In Musk's future, owners of the as yet unnamed space Tesla – roughly the size of a model X – would be blasted into a sub-orbital trajectory where speeds of up to Mach 7 would be possible, owing to an almost complete absence of air resistance. It opens the possibility of 'driving' from London to Sydney in a little over two hours.

'We are the right people to do this,' he said. 'We build cars, we build spacecraft. Henry Ford thought the car and the airplane would be combined; we think it's the car and the rocket.'

The 'sub-orbital' idea has been proposed before, notably by British Aerospace in the early 1980s. But their 'Hotol' (Horizontal Take-off and Landing) concept was an airliner seating several hundred people and operating to a schedule.

'The future of transport is personal,' says Musk. 'It always has been. Our concept would make the longest journeys currently possible on Earth simple day trips for regular car owners.'

The launch is the most challenging part of Musk's vision as it would require owners to report at a local site where their cars would be mated to a reusable rocket-powered 'sled'. 'But we're talking small ones,' Musk emphasises. 'We're only sending a car up, and it doesn't have to go into proper orbit. It's not as hard as it sounds.'

The landing would be relatively easy. Experience with SpaceX and rockets that can land themselves would be applied to the car. 'It would touch down autonomously – we know about that as well – even on a high street or in a parking lot. Then you would just drive away, normally.'

There is no indication yet of how much such a car would cost, apart from Musk's assertion that it would be 'not as much as you think'. There would be a hefty fee for a sub-orbital launch but, as Musk points out, 'We pay a fortune once or twice a year to fly our families somewhere on holiday. Spend that on a launch instead and enjoy your own car when you arrive.'

I look forward to the day when I can register my 'car' as a 'spacecraft'.

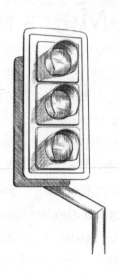

The Mutt's nuts

Ask anyone this side of Dr Johnson to define 'irony' and they'll find it pretty difficult. Give the job to some slightly dysfunctional Brummie custom bike builders and they'll have it nailed quicker than you can say it.

I'm talking about Mutt Motorcycles. They take Chinese licence-built versions of small Suzukis (the sort of Japanese bike that helped demolish the British motorcycle industry in the 1960s and 1970s) and convert them, using their own parts, into evocations of the British scrambler and home-made café racer of those far-off glory days, but with a digital gear indicator and Euro 4 compliance. They do this, obviously, in a building once occupied by BSA.

One part of me is uneasy with this sort of thing. Like the Royal Family, regional Cornish pasties and Oxfordshire, it smacks of an inability to move on. But on the other hand . . .

Mutt makes small motorcycles, 125s and 250s, with the avowed aim of getting people back into bikes. They may be on to something because they started a few years ago making a handful of these things, but now they're selling like, well, fashionable and reasonably priced, small capacity motorcycles. They're a bit hipster, you see.

It's weird. My own personal round-town weapon is a Honda MSX 125 (Grom, if you're in America), which is the sort of angular contemporary bike ridden by gangs of teenage yobbos around Japanese cities. I like that. Ride the Mutt and you can feel your beard growing. You will soon form the opinion that vinyl is so much 'warmer' than CDs or MP3 files. Eventually, you will give in and buy an open-face Davida and some goggles.

And it's obviously cool. When I ride my Repsol-liveried Fireblade, no one gives a toss. When I'm out on the Mutt, everyone wants to talk to me about it. Not only old farts who like to tell me how they rode all the way back from Liverpool on the back rim of their Norton 500 Thunderchuff; da kidz as well.

What I have here is the Hilts 250, inspired by Steve McQueen's bike in *The Great Escape*. So now it's customised Chinese licence-built Japanese technology posing as a 1960s 650 Triumph that was masquerading as a 1930s Wehrmacht BMW and actually ridden by Bud Ekins for the famous jump, in case McQueen face-planted it and lost his fortune. But let's not get bogged down.

Mutt designs a prototype, in this case based on the old Suzuki GN250. The Chinese factory builds around 65 per cent of the bike, then ships it to the UK where Mutt does all the nice bits: bars, lights, wheels, knobbly tyres, tank, seats, paintwork and what have you. There is a range of Mutt bikes, but they will combine the bits in any way you want. This is one of the advantages of working in 1950s Birmingham, away from the constraints of ruthlessly efficient, modern lean production methods.

Hip they may be, but Mutt's modifications make a great deal of sense for a biffabout bike that will, I suspect, largely be ridden about town. Not much point in riding it out in the wilds, because no one will see how goddam on-trend you're being. The low seat and wide bars make the riding position upright and comfortable – good for looking around, if only at your reflection in a window. It's very arse-steerable and reasonably light. Throw in a farty exhaust pipe and some noisy knobblies and the soundtrack comes good as well. Colour schemes from before the era of colour TV round off its retro cred.

To be honest, this isn't the most modern bike in the world. The GN lump is ancient and there's a bit of backlash in the transmission, which in turn is exacerbated by the lumpy one-pot power delivery. Sometimes, the shift from first to second makes a noise like Blue Öyster Cult's cowbell. Those tyres can feel a bit squirmy at low speeds. But so what? That's just enough authenticity, thanks, and it's balanced out by electric start, decent brakes, proper lights and all the other appurtenances of gracious living.[6]

I ended up being quite fond of the Mutt. At around £3700 (depends on your exact spec) it's no more

---

[6] © Quentin Willson, *Top Gear* (1991–2001).

expensive than a mainstream commuter bike or posh scooter, but while some of those can feel a bit humdrum, the Hilts does at least have proper character. It's amusing and it's strangely companionable.

It is, in fact, a bit like getting a dog.

A warning from history

The other day, I drove an original Honda NSX.

A bit of ancient history first. I started working on car magazines in 1990, as a sub-editor on *Autocar*. I was later fired. But one week we had the new and incredibly exciting NSX in for test, and one evening I was allowed to take it home.

This car, it was touted at the time, would be as exotic as the then Ferrari rival (the 348, not regarded as one of Fezza's better efforts) but over a third cheaper, and as reliable and easy to drive as a Civic. At the time, 'reliability' in Italian exotica was still something of a nebulous concept, and they had a reputation for being hard work. The gearbox wouldn't work properly until its oil had warmed up, for example.

But none of this meant anything to me. Firstly, I was a sub, not a road tester, so I was pretty low down the class system for driving the cars, although I had tried a Civic. I was also only twenty-seven. And I'd never driven a mid-engined car before, not even a Fiat X1/9, nor anything so rare and valuable.

I drove around in it pretty much all night, and I loved it. I was so mesmerised I didn't even think to go and pick up my then girlfriend in it. I simply drove around England in a youthful stupor of disbelief.

It really was pretty easy to drive, and when I was allowed a day in a Mondial some months later, I was amazed at how much 'management' it seemed to need. The Honda really did knock over many of the assumptions about supercar ownership.

Many things happened. I was fired from lots of other magazines, I drove and even owned innumerable mid-engined cars, and then found myself in 2016 with the new NSX. But there, at our track, was also a perfectly preserved original, brought along for illustrative purposes. Well, I had to have a go in that.

It was like stumbling across an album I'd loved as a student.

It was crap. It didn't help that it was an automatic, because even a Japanese automatic from the early 1990s changes gear with the conviction of me at the edge of a high diving board. It was also cumbersome, roly poly, heavy and dull in the steering, and quite unbelievably slow. Driving the new NSX was as undemanding and pleasurable as balancing a pencil on your fingertip. The old one was like carrying a suitcase.

Should have known, of course. Never meet your heroes, especially not those from formative periods of your life. It's why I never wanted to meet Derek Griffiths or Brian Cant. By the age of twenty-seven, I was fully formed in that I had two testicles, my voice had broken and I shaved, but I was woefully incomplete as a car enthusiast. That's why the NSX made such a huge and memorable impression on me in 1990. It lived in my mind like the vision of Catherine Anderson when I saw her naked in 1984. But I haven't seen her since.

This is at the root of my growing inner conflict about old cars. Car history is fascinating, because it's about so much more than cars. It's about society, humanity, our dreams and misplaced conceits, global power struggles and our often comedic vision of how we thought the future would be. Car styling is similarly fascinating because it's an important part of the history of art and design.

But you don't want to drive old cars. They're just not very good. It's that simple.

I went to work on the bus

Richard Hammond lives 130 miles from our office. I live 1.6. There are benefits to Hammond in all this; he has a much bigger and nicer house than me, more garden, better and more scenic roads for driving and riding bikes, immediate access to the land of daffodils, and much higher exposure to rustic home-made chutney and wife-carrying competitions.

On the other hand, I can go to work on the bus. I suppose Hammond could, technically, in the same way that I could walk to India, but it would take him a bit.

Meanwhile, I walk to the end of the road, get on the bus, swipe my debit card on the magic circle and, for a quid, ride all the way to the workplace. It's a bit 1950s (ignoring the swipe card) but it works; if there's a car for me to take away from work and try out, I avoid 'vehicle scatter' with my own stuff.

I have to be sure to get on the right bus, because dozens use that stop – there's a massive chart on all sides of a post, meaning I have to do a maypole dance to work out which one I need. If I get the wrong one, I look up from iPhone battleships and find myself in an uncharted world of inter-war housing that I didn't know existed. Then I have to work out which bus to catch to get myself back on course. And it's a lifetime's work.

On the whole, though, I like it. On a grim day like today, when the sky gleams like mercury,[7] it's low cost, comforting and pleasantly communal. Clarkson would claim that it will give me a disease, or that I'll be murdered by a lunatic, but so far this hasn't happened. No industrial-era bronchial disorder has been transmitted to me by a young mother and her child, and I've checked my torso for the handles of knives sticking out. There aren't any.

Clarkson is also fond of quoting Margaret Thatcher,

[7] Ivor Cutler, God rest him.

she who (allegedly) said, 'Any man who, beyond the age of twenty-six, finds himself on a bus can count himself as a failure.'

But here am I, aged fifty-three, with a happy life and an interesting job, and I have my own Ferrari. So I'm forced to conclude that Margaret Thatcher was talking crap.

Power, torque, finally

There has never been as much crap talked within a single arena of human interest as has been talked amongst car enthusiasts on the subject of power and torque.

I thought I'd have a crack at explaining them to anyone who doesn't get it. I realise this might come out as a bit simplistic if you're an engineer or physicist and you do get it, but in that case, you won't be reading this anyway. Anyone else, keep going. Also, there won't be any calculations in this, because we're concerned only with conceptual understanding. And numbers make people reach for a service revolver with a single round in it.

The first thing to understand is that torque is simply a force; a force like the one you apply pushing a broken-down Alfa Romeo off the road. It's a slightly confusing force because it works in a circular sort of way instead of a straight line, but we needn't worry about that too much. If you like, think of trying to undo a nut with a spanner. How hard you push and how long the spanner is are both significant. So torque is (think of the units, like lb-ft) a force at a distance.

The second thing to understand is that power is defined (in physics) as 'the rate of doing work'. So there you go. Torque is the size of the job you can do, power is how quickly you can do it. To be honest, we can leave it at that. I would.

You want more? I got it, brothers and sisters, and here it comes.

A car engine can't produce anything unless it's running. Once it's running – the crankshaft is spinning round and round – it is producing power and torque. The two are inseparable, and anything else you may have heard has come straight from the horse's arse.[8]

Because the crankshaft is turning, it is producing

---
[8] Electric motors and steam engines are slightly different. Leave it . . .

that mysterious circular force mentioned above. Because it is turning at a speed, it's capable of applying that force at a certain rate, which is the definition of power. Power is torque multiplied by engine speed.

So power allows you to do work at a certain rate, and let's say the job in hand is accelerating out of a tight bend. Here, 300 horsepower is 300 horsepower. It could be reached by a high torque engine turning quite slowly, or an engine with puny torque turning very quickly. That 'torque times speed' thing works out the same. So the torque and power curves you see on those graphs can be manipulated, and that's what leads to 'engine characteristics', but they're both going to be there.

Something else worth remembering. An engine with 500 horsepower has that as its peak power. It doesn't give that everywhere. In modern engines the power peak generally occurs just before the rev limiter is reached; in old racing engines, just before the whole thing disintegrates.

An engine with 350lb ft of torque generates that at its peak, too. Not everywhere. In modern engines, with electronic ignition and injection control, variable valve timing and so on, that torque peak might be spread quite lavishly throughout a broad part of the rev range. On older engines, such as a small capacity Japanese racing bike engine from the 1960s, it is often a fleeting thing, like the beauty of the cherry blossom.

But wherever there is torque, there is also power, and power cannot exist without torque, because it would have nothing to give. Torque and power, together, are a sanctified union the division of which leaves both parts purposeless, like John Donne and his mistress.

We are now at the edge of a terrifying abyss at the bottom of which is the reason for needing a gearbox. Do you want that too, or are you ready to end it all?

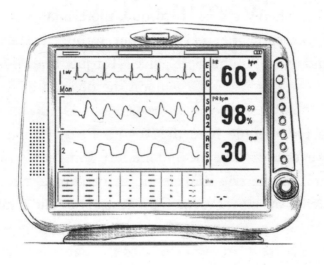

Warning: Toyota Prius review

A lot of people hate the Toyota Prius. When you drive one, as I've now done for some 600 miles, other people will make a point of overtaking you, instead of just overtaking. Some people cleverly refer to it as the 'pious', which doesn't really work, as the correct pronunciation of the name is Pree-us, not Pry-us.

It's widely assumed that if you drive a Prius you are some sort of evangelist for a new utopian age, but maybe a lot of them are simply being driven by people who like sensible cars that don't use too much fuel. Just a thought. 'Or Uber drivers,' comes the cry. So? They're chosen by people who drive for a living and are playing a decisive part in the general rethink of personal transport. Not much of a criticism.

Clarkson has dismissed this car as 'a cynical marketing exercise' aimed at faux environmentalists, and I can see where he's coming from, but I'm not so sure. Toyota, being the far-sighted lot that they are, started work on the Prius in 1968, which was before the environment had been invented. I'm inclined to think that Toyota realised the electric motor would have a place in the future of the car, but that it wasn't ready to be let out on its own, because battery technology hadn't really progressed since the days when Baker Electrics roamed the streets of the USA. And let's not forget that Japanese car makers have always been interested in fuel efficiency. It's why they triumphed in that difficult 1970s crisis period.

In any case, I'm not really that interested in the environment. I'm so sad, I'm actually interested in drivetrains. The trouble with this is that properly understanding the one in the Prius is a bit like trying to translate dial-up modem into English, and once you start taking an interest you find yourself dragged into a descending vortex to acronym hell, where

Beelzebub will have the following warmed up for you on the end of a toasting fork: ICE, MG1, MG2, HVB, eCVT, HSD, ECU, WTF. This is only the beginning of your torment. Delve further and you quickly become a victim of Continually Repeated Acronym Phenomenon.

Let's move on. I'm going to stick my neck out and say I quite like the way the Prius (and indeed many other recent offerings from Toyota and Lexus) looks. As a whole, and from some angles, it seems a bit clumsy, but it's full of interesting styling details and definitely looks Japanese, or possibly a bit like Hannibal Lecter when he had his muzzle on.

You would, however, struggle to say the Prius is exciting to drive. The performance is absolutely average, the handling is benign, the ride is sort of normal. Some aspects of it seem a bit old-fashioned, such as the touchscreen display. When this is having a digital think, it flashes up the legend: 'I'm working on it . . .' This is a bit like having a celebrity voice on your sat-nav; not really very funny from the off, and quickly leading to murderous ill temper.

What the Prius is, however, is interesting.

There are lots of things to look at on the fascia. There are a lot of things on the fascia of, say, an Audi, too, but there's something strangely mesmerising about all the information in the Prius, especially the energy flow display, because you can amuse yourself trying to make the battery recharge or the engine cut in and out and . . . shit! I haven't looked out of the windscreen for what feels like half an hour.

You can move the oddly appealing shift lever into B on downhill stretches and on the approach to junctions, giving you enhanced regenerative braking, and this becomes a good game in itself; trying to avoid using the brakes. Good idea, as the real brakes are a bit grabby. It's like an absurd video game with points as prizes in the form of a commendable consumption graph (Look out of the bloody window!) and you can inadvertently turn into a hypermiler while trying to amuse yourself on a long and lonely commute. Perhaps it's a plot.

In very mixed driving on motorways, A-roads and small lanes, much of it like a bit of an arse to be honest, I achieved an overall 60.2mpg, which you might manage with a modern diesel. But then you'd be driving a diesel. The distant moan of the Prius's petrol engine, CVT transmission and drive motor are a more contemporary sort of sound, I think.

Look, it's just a car. In a way, the banality of the Prius is a measure of its success. It was not the first hybrid car – the idea is almost as old as the car itself – but it is probably the most significant. Without it, we would not have arrived so quickly at hybrid supercars and the hybrid racing cars running at Le Mans. If some successor of mine makes another *Cars of the People* TV series in thirty years' time, the Prius should be in it. Whether we like it or not.

Reviewed: junk

I hesitate to say this on a forum like DriveTribe. This isn't, I suspect, going to be a very popular view, although that isn't a problem because the point of DriveTribe is to start a fight. And being unpopular isn't the same as being wrong.

We're going to have to accept that old cars are rubbish, even the E-type Jag. Sorry about this, but few subjects occupy such a lofty position in the bollocksphere as cars, and largely because so many people think they were better in the olden days.

They weren't, and we can arrive at this conclusion through simple and unassailable logic, without the hindrance of emotion or any subjective nonsense. Allow me.

Back in the 1990s, my dad complained that cars were better in the 1970s. But now I meet people, often on here, who think cars were better in the 1990s, which comes as a bit of a surprise, because I thought they were supposed to be boring and they all looked the same.

So at any point in time there is a disturbingly large number of people who believe cars were better twenty or thirty years ago. But that would mean cars have been in decline ever since Bertha Benz complained that this new Ford Model T wasn't half as good as her old man's Motorwagen was. It can't possibly be true.

It's a bit like the old argument that the world is going to the dogs. Every generation says it, but if it were true we'd have arrived at the dogs many centuries ago. We haven't.

New cars are obviously better made and better equipped. They are also safer, cleaner and more dependable. They are more affordable to more people in real terms. They are a better expression of the state of new technology than they've ever been. Most importantly – and this is the bit that will annoy everyone – they're better to drive.

They just are. I recently drove a basic Mk1 Golf, and what a dismal Soviet-spec experience that was, with its pig-iron suspension, biscuit-tin build, and single banal instrument mocking me from the fascia for the feeble ambition of its age. If you honestly think this is better, then you must think a twin-tub, top-loading washing machine is better than the one that allows you to simply throw your pants through the door and then go to the pub. Do you?

Look, I get it. Old cars arc fascinating, and nothing reveals the conceit of nations and individual people quite like the history of the car. I've made two series on the subject for TV. It's gripping stuff, but the cars themselves are no longer any good.

I'd like to sign off, before you finish building the gallows, by saying that I'm glad other people are interested in old cars and drive around in them. I've always maintained that the best car museum in the world is the one out on the road, because it's all very well going to stare at car history at Beaulieu, but not half as exciting as coming across something interesting out on the street.

I mean, a few weeks ago, driving through town in

my thoroughly modern BMW, I saw a man parking up a mint 1970s Cadillac Seville, a car I remember reading about when I was a lad. It looked amazing.

I bet it was shit, though.

Reviewed: being an arse

While I was away on holiday, and therefore not paying attention, something odd happened. The British government starting a consultation into a proposed new law, to cover 'death by dangerous cycling'.

Cycling groups were up in arms, and I'm with them. For years various 'action groups' have campaigned for bicycles to be registered, for bicycles to pay road tax, for bicycles to pass a roadworthiness test, blah blah blah, but it's all the hollow rantings of people who think the world's ills can be cured with paperwork.

And in any case, if someone is capable of riding a bicycle in such a batshit way that they can knock down and kill someone (it's happened, sadly), then isn't there already a law to cover that? There would be in May's Britain, because it would come under 'Don't Be an Arse', which is the only law a completely civilised country needs.

This brings me to driving, where I find too much evidence that a lot of people are still in breach of the Arse ruling.

Here's the issue. When I were a lad, the car was the undisputed king. Nothing was allowed to impede it, and if you were run over by one then it was your fault for being in the way of social progress.

But that's all changed, and rightly so. The place of the car has been massively reassessed over the last decade, and it's come under scrutiny for undeniable offences: for the pollution it produces, for the noise and smell it makes, for the clutter it causes, for the resources it consumes, and for the congestion it creates. And because it runs over people, if you're not very careful.

In fact, I foresee that the end of cars will come not because of environmental concerns, but because it will become legally untenable to own and operate one. It therefore falls to us, as ambassadors for something that most people regard as a dreary necessity but that we love, to delay this dreadful day as long as possible. And I'm afraid that does mean not being an arse.

So, if the road is remote and open and the weather good, give it some beanage. I do. But no speeding in built-up areas, no wheelspin, no traffic-light drag races, no doughnuts in supermarket car parks, no loud pipes, and absolutely no drifting, even on the moon. And never, ever, blow the horn. Honda's motorcycle brochures used to include a little edict that said: 'Good roadcraft and courtesy identify the skilled and stylish rider.' That's how we need to be seen, as skilled and stylish, for the sake of our hobby.

Just so you know: in May's Britain there is only the one law and also only one punishment. All offenders are given the same size rock, plus a hammer, and a fine-grade sieve through which all the broken-up bits have to pass. The only thing that changes is the size of the hammer.

If you're a murderer or a rapist, you get one of those minuscule watchmakers' mallets, and you'll be there until you die. If you drove through the village a bit too quickly, you'll get a massive lump hammer and you'll be free by the end of the day.

Racing through the town centre and running over people? God, you've got a tiny tool.

Reviewed: buttocks

Years ago, I interviewed the chairman of Lego, who told me he wanted to turn the already highly successful brick-making colossus into a 'one buttock company'.

I was a bit baffled by this. He explained that he knew a concert pianist, and this pianist, while learning a new concerto or what not, would sit squarely on the piano stool. But he knew when he'd finally got to grips with the music because he was always sitting on one buttock or the other, but never both. That was a signifier of success, dynamism and generally moving forward. Perhaps Beethoven's *Emperor* was in his repertoire of one-buttock concertos.

Your butt, in fact, is a talented and very discerning

extremity. Driving is not that different from playing music, in that they're both performative activities. Now, though, your buns are a conduit of vital feedback rather than a passive confirmation that all is well.

The human/machine interface is a very complex area of study. We make inputs to driving the car – moving the gearstick, turning the wheel, pressing the brake pedal – and the car to a greater or lesser extent feeds back data on the effects. We have many sensory receptors, including the inner ear, fingertips, our viscera in general, pretty much everything. That includes your plum duff. You may not be aware of this, but believe me, you'd struggle to drive if you had no jacksie, as much as you would if blindfold.

We're talking here about your actual buttocks; the gluteus group of muscles, comprising maximus, minimus and medius. These pump information to the brain about balance and position when running, jumping or standing on the deck of a heaving boat. They are similarly active when driving a car. They also give you somewhere convenient to sit, and they're always there.

Back to autonomous cars, then. Obviously, they need some sort of feedback system so that the car's brain knows exactly what the car is doing at any moment in time. There's a lot of this sort of stuff on cars already, notably the accelerometers and such that govern traction control, four-wheel steering and so on. The autonomous car will need a lot more of this stuff if it is to respond with the precision and sophistication of the human body-brain.

What I'm saying is, artificial intelligence and machine learning are great, and vital. But for the autonomous car to be truly successful, it's going to need its own arse.

Reviewed: changing gear

A lot of people would understand that, in a petrol engine, a spark is needed to ignite the fuel and air mixture as the piston reaches the top of its compression stroke.

What many people don't realise – apologies to those of you who feel patronised – is that the spark doesn't always come at the same time. Sometimes it's a bit earlier, sometimes later, depending on what we're demanding of the engine: climbing a hill in a low gear, for example, is different from cruising at high speed in top.

Engineers call this variation in spark timing 'advance' and 'retard', and for a long time it's been done automatically. First it was triggered by changes in manifold pressure or spinning weights; more recently it's done by electronic systems that understand the situation in minute detail.

But there was a time, when Jeremy Clarkson was a teenager, when it had to be done manually, usually with a little lever on the steering wheel. You had to understand the effects of advance and retard to drive your car. But them days is long gone and nobody laments the passing of that bit of the control interface.

There are other bits of the car that have also long gone. A few that spring to mind are mixture control, the magneto/coil switch, manual oil and fuel pumps, engine primers, cranking handles and grease nipples. There are others that are on the way out, such as hand-wound windows and sunroofs. No one is sad about any of this.

But at the slightest suggestion that the manual gear-box and clutch are about to disappear, around half of DriveTribe is ready to march on the palace with blazing torches.

I get it, actually. I've often thought that those two controls are a vital part of feedback. As the car rushes towards a corner it becomes somehow expansive, but then as you brake and select a lower gear, it sort of gathers itself up and becomes smaller, like a cat preparing to pounce. But now I've decided I prefer paddles.

I'm in the lucky position of owning cars with both. But these days, when I'm driving the manual, I feel almost affronted. You want me to do that myself? With that ridiculous stick thing? You want me to interrupt and then reconnect the drive? With my leg? Don't be daft.

Paddles are just better. It's still about changing gear, and when is still up to you, which is what matters. But now it's all in the fingertips, which is the true conduit for our understanding of the tactile world, and so the experience is purer. It's why motorcycles are so satisfying: the controls requiring the greatest sensitivity – throttle, clutch and front brake – are in your hands.

Put it this way. If you blindfolded yourself to heighten the pleasure of discovering the subtleties in the curvature of your loved one's buttocks, you wouldn't then do it with your foot.

One day, pretty soon, the manual gearbox will fade away. No one will give a toss. And then, when we're all driving electrically, the gearbox will disappear completely. No one will give a toss about that, either. Move on.

Reviewed: drivers' cars

There are a lot of people out there who claim that unless you drive a manual car with no ABS or traction control, then you're not a real driver at all. You're just a 'steering wheel monkey'.

Driver aids, so their thinking goes, are breeding a generation of motoring pumice stones, unable to absorb the sensations through which the true helmsperson expresses the artistry of driving; unable to take proper responsibility for driving the car and instead handing important decisions to someone in an R&D lab watched over by a safety Nazi. But hang on a minute.

I wonder how many of them have driven a car

without synchromesh? Go back a generation and you could find people who would decry this pitiable driver aid that allows you to change gear at the wrong time. That, in essence, is what synchromesh does. If you really understand your gearbox, and can commune fully with its cussed, whirling character, you should be able to drive around all day without using the clutch at all. Can you do this? No? Pussy.

That, of course, is assuming you know where the gears are in the first place. For a long time, they were outside, and even when they were inside, first might be where you think fourth should be, and the throttle could be the middle pedal. In a Ford Model T, lifting what you imagine is the clutch might make you go backwards, although this depends on the position of what you assumed was the handbrake. So we're pretty chuffed about the standardised layout of all the main controls. Bunch of thin yoghurts.

There are countless features on proper drivers' cars that, at some point, would have been considered mere sops to the witless. The brake servo, for example, which is welcome if you're the sort of snowflake who likes stopping in time. Brakes, in fact, since they weren't always a given. What about the steering wheel? Early cars had tillers, like boats, but everyone soon saw the logic behind the analogue proportionality of the round thing. What a bunch of jessies.

Radial tyres? You must be a right wus if you assume that the rubber will grip the road rather than fall off the rim. Headlights that give a focused beam of white light rather than the diffused jar-of-piss tint seen in old photographs? What on earth is wrong with everyone? A roof for when it rains? We really are a bunch of soft shites. Ignition advance? Differentials? Electric starters? Engine-driven oil pumps? I'm amazed we can still dress ourselves.

My point is thus: whether or not a refinement is an intrusive driver aid or simply an integral part of what a car is assumed to be depends on where you stand in the timespan of history. We happen to be in the present, and the process isn't complete yet.

I know we're all living in fear of the rise of the driverless car, and automated systems are coming thick and fast. But let me assure you of this. For the foreseeable future, aeroplanes will be flown by pilots, and cars will be driven by drivers.

Guten abend

Every decade or so (in Britain at least) the electric toothbrush goes through a renaissance. It started in the 1970s and we're having one at the moment.

The electric toothbrush is always touted as the cure-all solution to every oral hygiene issue, and millions are sold and discussed in cafés, but then they're forgotten for a bit. Then they come back. What you need is an electric toothbrush.

They used to oscillate from side-to-side. Then they went round and round, back and forth. Now the one I've bought oscillates from side to side again. Hang on? Isn't that what they were like when I was a lad?

This could continue into the age of teleportation and living on Pluto, so we need to decide once and for all. Is the electric toothbrush A Thing, or just a load of old bollocks?

It's a load of old bollocks.

Good. Now we can move on to the naked motorcycle. This also comes and goes to some extent, and for a while we have been in the positive phase of the yes/no naked motorcycle. I have one, a BMW R nineT.

In some ways, I ought to disapprove of it. Despite being perfectly modern in engineering terms, it's a bit retro. Thing is, it's a retro philosophy rather than a completely retro look, being a BMW boxer-based special. But it's built like that in the factory, instead of being produced from an old R80 under the arches by a slightly subversive outfit called something like Fucknuckle's Chop-Shop.

Cheating, then. Building specials out of boxer BMWs has been in vogue for ages. The bikes are plentiful, they're German-made and robust, easy to mess with and they look cool. So by doing it like this from the start, BMW are denying a job to people with un-corporate hairstyles and tats of crossed pistons on their forearms.

I suppose you could be really bloody-minded and make a special out of the special. BMW have done that as well. First they did a scrambler version of the R nineT, and now there's this, the R nineT Racer, kindly loaned to me by the blokes from Bahnstormer (who, by the way, make their own specials of all these specials, with amazing paint schemes, wacko headlights, etc., etc., etc. Where will it end?).

It's basically the same bike but with a different front end: different forks and bars, and that old-skool cyclops fairing. BMW Motorsport graphics, too. Nice. The forks and brakes have been downgraded a bit from the 'standard' R nineT bits, which seems odd as this is the 'racer', but it looks handsome.

A few things are immediately apparent. The engine – actually the old air/oil cooled GS and RT engine, before those bikes went all liquid-cooled and revvy – is full of wonderful character, encouraging you to short-shift and enjoy the good vibrations. The tank is a lovely shape, and because you lean right over it, there are more opportunities (although you'll do this with all

Boxer BMWs) to look down and marvel at the cylinders sticking out on either side of the engine. What are they doing there? They're not so much part of the bike as travelling along in formation with it.

The other thing I noticed is that this bike seems incredibly long. It is, by the standards of modern sports bikes. This means it's nice 'n' stable and therefore surprisingly relaxing at speed, but the front wheel does seem an awfully long way away and the steering is something that happens in the future. That means it's a bit ponderous if you're jammin' through heavy traffic, and looking behind you is harder because, well, you're almost lying down.

In the end, I was a bit unsure. It's a lovely thing and allows owners to entertain fantasies about being Karlheinz Scheisskopf, who rode to an unexpected victory in the 1972 Grand Prix of Rothosen on a BMW Zweithumpheren.[9] But it's a bit too knowing for my tastes, and slightly hard work. I ended up yearning for my own R nineT, a no-nonsense motorcycle-shaped bike that chugs about and can be steered with my pelvis. This was all a bit serious. And anyway,

---

[9] Completely made up.

Richard Hammond really likes it, which renders it unutterably unacceptable.

I've decided I don't want the special special. I want the standard special.

How to draw a car

There are many good reasons for building a so-called 'mid-engined' supercar, but one of the most compelling is to do with something called 'polar inertia'. Don't panic. What this physics teachery expression means is simply 'resistance to turning'.

As much of the mass as possible is positioned near the middle of the car, because that means it will change direction more willingly. Imagine carrying a ladder horizontally, and trying to turn around. If you hang a pot of paint on each end, it's quite hard; but if you hang the two pots of paint in the middle, it's much easier. The weight of the paint pots is still the same, but it's more centralised. Pots on ends, high polar inertia: pots in middle, low polar inertia. There you go.

This thinking came from racing, of course, where it confers many competitive advantages. Apart from being more lively, the mid-engined layout lends itself to equal front and rear weight distribution. Less weight at the front gives the steering tyres an easier time in the bends, too. A bit more weight towards the back aids traction coming out of them.

As well as putting the weight towards the middle, it makes sense to put it as low down as possible as well. This reduces the tendency for roll in bends, which does more to save tyres and gives the suspension less to cope with. So the driver and passenger sit low down.

A dry-sump engine can be mounted a bit lower than a wet-sump one, because, well, there's less sump to squeeze in. Even using a flat-plane crankshaft can make a small difference. Cross-plane cranks need bigger balancer webs, which makes the crankcase a bit deeper. It all adds up. Or, rather, takes away.

And all of the above helps with aerodynamics, because you can have a car with a low frontal area and a pointy nose – no engine to squeeze in up there.

So: the basic shape of the mid-engined supercar is largely dictated by a few facts of physics. This is one of the reasons they appeal. They look the way they do for sound engineering reasons. They just happen to look brilliant as well.

But now what? Electric supercars are upon us and they don't have to accommodate an engine or a gearbox or even a fuel tank. The batteries can go in the floor and the (relatively small) electric motors can go in each wheel. Aerodynamics are still a huge consideration, of course, but even they are liberated in this scenario.

So for the first time since the Lotus Europa and the Lamborghini Miura, the supercar doesn't need to look the way it does. The shapes of electric supercars seen so far are a hangover from the mid-engined philosophy, because that's how we expect them to look.

The question is, what should they look like? I've no real idea.

The silence of the amps

There are people who think electric cars are dangerous, because pedestrians can't hear them coming. But
I think this is nonsense.

European legislators agree, though, because from
now on, new EVs must emit a noise 'similar' to that of
an internal combustion engine, at a volume of 56dB,
when travelling below 20kph. US legislators also agree,
although they've set the limit at 30kph, perhaps
because Americans take longer to react. It's still
nonsense.

Firstly, this ruling is clearly aimed at improving
pedestrian safety in towns, but the beauty of EVs is
that they will make towns much quieter, which means

better sleep, more agreeable pavement cafés, and a general improvement in wellbeing. What is the point of, finally, achieving what Rolls-Royce has been attempting for over a century – a silent car – and then adding a fake noise to it? If all IC cars are replaced by EVs but they all emit 56dB in town, we'll be back where we started.

I have a more serious objection, though. As a pedestrian, it is not your responsibility not to be run over. As a driver, it's your job not to run over people. If you cross the road without looking, you're a bit of a plonker, but if you're driving, you should expect people to do it. If you support the idea of an Audible Vehicle Alert System you're basically saying you rely on the noise a car makes to keep pedestrians safe. That's not really good enough.

Charities for the blind are pleased with this new law, and I get that. But I haven't heard much from the deaf (not intended as a joke). If you can't hear at all, then even the noise made by a 1960s American muscle car isn't going to help you.

I've been saying for years that what we actually need – what all new cars need, as most conventional cars are pretty quiet at low speeds – is some sort of polite horn.

The other day, for example, I was driving my EV out in the sticks and came up behind a woman walking her dog in the middle of the road. She hadn't heard me. So now what was I to do? I couldn't blow the normal horn, because that would be unbelievably rude and might have given her a heart attack. So I had to follow her at 2mph until the dog needed a poo and she turned off into the hedgerows.

What I really needed was a horn that made a discreet 'ahem' sound, or maybe a donkey honk, or even a few bars of Michael Bubbly, because that's enough. If it also emitted a strong but low-frequency vibration, maybe deaf people could also 'hear' it.

Here's a thought. Tesla famously equips its cars with a hilarious device for making fart noises come out of the passenger seats when you press one of the steering wheel buttons. Very funny, Elon.

Would be a lot more useful on the outside of the car.

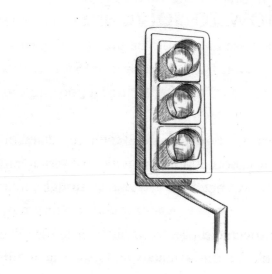

How to solve F1

How do we sort out Formula 1? Elsewhere, Clarkson argues that wings should be banned, and it's not a bad idea. But first, we need to answer a fundamental question.

Is F1 a pure spectacle, or a technology crucible? I've decided it should be the latter because, as it is, it can never be good to watch. Professional drivers are too consistent, and we know before the race which is the fastest car/driver combination. So the only thing that changes the result is a cock-up, a breakdown, or some dreary tactical stuff about changing tyres.

But don't worry, because F1 as a technological struggle will be a good laugh.

Here are my rules. The first is that there are no rules, because innovation does not permit them. Progress belongs to anarchic and unreasonable people, not conformists. I would limit the length and width of the car, and the total energy consumption (in Joules), but that's it. Anything else goes. Steam power, if you can make it work.

My second rule is that there can be no team drivers. Instead, each week, the drivers are selected at random from the public using a system similar to British jury service; that is, a letter arrives, and unless you're in prison, a student or about to give birth, you have to drive for McLaren for a week. Testing, practice, qualifying. It's the law.

Pre-race interviews are already much more interesting, because they're with a plumber, a baker, an accountant and a retired woodwork teacher, any of whom will earn £1 million if they win. Rooting for the affable builders' merchant from Manchester when your mate wants the Japanese chef to win is all part of the fun.

This is a great stimulus to the constructors. They will have to design a whole range of cars, and which one they field will depend on what sort of driver they get. The need for absolute performance will have to be weighed against usability, because you might get Lewis Hamilton on Driver Service but you might get me, or my dad. Driver aids are permitted, which will help with the development of the autonomous car, and safety will have to be of the utmost importance, because you can't kill the general public in the name of sport.

Finally, F1 is relevant. It's still about performance, but of a sort applicable to the car you actually buy. It has to be, because you might be driving. More to the point, next year's Belgian Grand Prix might be won by a seamstress from Delhi.

You want to watch that, don't you?

Speeding fine, blah blah blah

I was recently busted by a speed camera for doing 37mph in a 30mph limit. To be honest, that stretch of 30mph seems absurd (it used to be 40mph) and I know that camera catches a lot of people. I could go on to say that it looks like a cynical money-grabbing exercise.

But I'm pretty bored with motoring journalists banging on about speed cameras. It's been going on for at least twenty years. The fact is that there was a sign, the camera was yellow, and there were those photogrammetry lines on the road. I wasn't really paying attention. I cocked up.

Annoying, really, because I try my best to stick to

urban speed limits. Most of them are fair enough. But I'm only human and I make mistakes.

So do you. So does everyone who drives, including the righteous members of road safety groups and anti-speed campaigns. 'Well, you were caught,' comes the cry. But the offence is not being caught, the offence is speeding.

So, morally, everyone who drives must immediately go down the cop shop and hand themselves in. But that isn't going to happen, and we can't have a society that makes everyone a criminal, because it would become meaningless.

And in any case, a lot of people will simply have made a mistake. We arrive here at a complicated philosophical conundrum – making mistakes is the lot of humanity, and legislating against that is nonsense.

Here's a suggestion. We can have speed cameras, we continue to paint them yellow and all the rest of it. But you can speed, say, six times in a year before you get a fine. But you don't know how many times you've been caught until you've done it six times and you get the letter.

Sounds tyrannical, doesn't it? But it's perfectly fair, because it goes some way to distinguishing between people who have merely erred occasionally and those for whom it's a genuine bad habit. And let's say you get a written warning after the first three.

The point of speed cameras, we're told, is to stop people speeding. This system still does, but avoids the moral effrontery of punishing them for being human.

Tell me why I'm wrong, please.

Reviewed: stop-start

A lot of you youngsters these days seem to have quite nice cars. Fairly new ones. But it wasn't like that when I was a lad. We drove old shit, and it often didn't work.

If a car is running, then according to something deeply ingrained in my driving conscience, that is a bonus. It follows, therefore, that when it stops running at a set of traffic lights, it's broken. That's how it was for so many years.

Look, stop-start is a perfectly reasonable idea. As I've said before on this tribe, the internal combustion engine has to idle before it can do anything useful, unlike an electric motor or a steam engine. But it need only start idling in the instant before you call on it. If you're stationary, it can be turned off.

It's not even a new idea. Twenty-five years ago, long before electronic systems took over the job, I noticed that the taxi drivers of Calcutta would turn their engines off at traffic lights. Made sense; it saved a bit of fuel, and the Hindustan Ambassador was designed by Richard Trevithick, and made a bit of a stink. But it did seem a bit ill-advised to a man still traumatised by a 130,000-mile and unserviced Vauxhall.

Even now I sense a tiny kernel of panic forming in my bowels whenever the car turns itself off at a junction. It's like a very mild form of shell shock; a trigger for the memory of some horror in a previous life. Who's to say it will start again, when for so many decades it almost certainly wouldn't?

But there's something else. I was driving a Land Rover Discovery, with the stop-start turned on. It stopped when I pulled up at a pedestrian crossing, and because I was unconsciously applying a tiny force to the steering wheel, I felt the power steering fade away and the wheel become inert. I felt a car die. It was like a beloved pet expiring in my arms, and it was horrible, and I hated it.

That's why every car I've ever driven with stop-start has a button that allows you to switch the system out. There's no reason to have this that I can think of, except that it's there for my generation. But it will pass away, like the idea of almshouses. And then we will be at peace.

Tree huggers – cheers

Do you know what? Those wacko greenies were right all along, although possibly not for the reasons they thought. The issue is not about saving the Earth, it's about saving humanity, and 'sustainability' is really about sustaining our happiness.

While we're all getting exercised about the proposed ban on petrol and diesel cars, it might be worth considering that this is something of a specific. So internal combustion will fade away, but so what? Future generations will lament its demise no more than I lament the end of bear-baiting.

Our worry about the acceptability of the car is merely one way of expressing a more general concern about our continued contentment. There is a bigger picture, so here's the usual one.

Human happiness, according to my mate Dan, is about 'a nice life full of stuff that works'. He may be on to something, and I think it will come down to three things: the provision of ample food, recyclability and abundant, harmless energy.

I'm going to put the food bit to one side, like an overdone sprout, because I don't know anything about that. But here goes with everything else.

As humans, we like to create and produce. Doesn't matter whether it's growing some roses or designing and manufacturing a new computer. It makes us happy and gives us gainful employment. We also like to consume because it incrementally improves our lives. But at the same time, we worry that in doing these things we are filling the world with crap.

But if everything is totally and infinitely recyclable, this doesn't matter, because your car or your phone or your floral sports jacket are merely the current hosts of materials that will soon become something else, and then something else after that. All our industrious urges met, without filling the sea with polythene.

This, however, demands limitless energy, which means all efforts towards renewables, nuclear fusion, antimatter and dilithium are wholly commendable. One of these energy sources will find its way into your car, probably in the form of electricity, but where it has come from, who knows? Let's not get bogged down in whether or not a plug-in rechargeable BMW or a fuel-cell Honda is actually 'green', it's all part of the investigation into a bigger solution.

So, there you go. Everything sorted. If cars are your particular thing, then you will have a new one more often, and it will be better than the last one while relieving you of guilt. Indeed, you will have a nice life full of stuff that works.

Off we go.

The gearbox explained

Be honest: have you ever looked at the rev counter in your car before changing gear? I don't think I have. Your bones know. Sound, vibrations and the magnitude of the tug on your intestines tell you which gear you need.

It follows, then, that everyone understands, instinctively, what the gearbox is for, and why most cars need one. But if you really do want an explanation, here it is.

Remember from my last essay on power and torque that (in simple terms) torque is the size of the job you can do, and power is how quickly you can do it. Power is a derived attribute equal to torque times engine speed. Hold that thought, in the form of your favourite biscuit, in your head.

Now we add the gearbox to the engine, and the gearbox can be thought of as a series of crowbars in circular, continuous form. You can use a crowbar to shift a boulder that you couldn't possibly move unaided. A longer crowbar makes it even easier, but you won't move the boulder as quickly.

Gears, like crowbars, are 'torque multipliers'. Let's say a gearbox ratio halves the speed of the engine crankshaft. That doubles the torque. But the power remains constant, because twice as much torque multiplied by half as much speed works out the same.

'Torque is the size of the job you can do.' The 'job', in a car, can range from a big 'un, such as accelerating from rest up a steep hill, to a light one, such as cruising at a steady 50mph on a level road when you get to the top.

So, pulling away. Loads of torque needed, to do the job of overcoming gravity and the car's inertia, to get it moving. You'll know what I mean if you've ever had to push your car. First gear, then.

Trouble is, you'll soon reach the engine's redline, even though the car isn't going very fast yet. But no matter, because the job is now smaller. Second gear then. Still quite a lot of torque, and the same power, but it's a shorter crowbar, so the speed is higher.

And so it goes on, until you're cruising on the flat, and the job is a simple matter of overcoming tyre and air resistance. So you're in the toppermost of gears, which gives you little torque but high speed, while keeping the engine in its ideal operating range. If you need to accelerate quickly from this point, you change down. The job has become bigger, so you need a helping dollop of torque. The engine speed will climb, too, to unacceptable levels. But now you're up to 90 and the job is done, so it's back into top for a long-legged loaf. Obviously I'm avoiding saying 'top gear' for complex socio/political reasons.

If you're still with me, and you haven't turned over to 'lol cars epic fails', then there's another way of thinking about this, which is a dockside crane unloading a container from the bowels of a cargo ship.

The container is very heavy, so the crane's engine is geared down to increase the torque, which is the force that raises the thing up. It comes up very slowly, though. But then if you wanted to unload something very small and light, like Richard Hammond, you could gear the crane up and he would come out of the hold like a jack-in-the-box, or a twat-in-a-ship.

That's gears for you. I hope this was useful.

Them's the rules

What are the rules of the road? In England, the most basic one is 'keep left', which is a pretty good convention and one that has prevented a lot of nasty surprises on winding country lanes. But in some parts of the world you've cocked this up and made it 'keep right', which is unhelpful, frankly.

So who's to say? Official rules of the road, the ones in government publications, tend to be pretty simple – which side to drive on, speed limits, the meanings of some signs, that sort of thing. But there is a deeper layer of 'rules' that are more akin to social niceties or manners. I don't think they're written down anywhere; they're broadly understood but a bit fluid. Hence road rage. Like all problems, it stems from incomplete understanding.

Here in England, it's generally accepted that if you want to make a significant manoeuvre – change lanes, say – then you wait for permission from those whom you might inconvenience. A flash of lights, or a wave perhaps. If you don't, you might be subjected to some tootling of the horn trumpet.[10]

India, where I've driven a bit, is different. If your car is ahead in the general melee, even if only by the depth of its front bumper, you're entitled to move in. That's how it seemed to me anyway, and I got along just fine.

Cairo: the horn is polite. It means 'I'm coming past', and not tootling it would be inconsiderate. In England, it generally means 'you bastard'. For that reason, polite English people never use it. Confusing, eh?

I've recently been to Colombia, and I didn't quite have time to work out the 'rules'. But I could make a new lane if there was space, and why not? I wouldn't do that at home. I'd be tootled to a pulp.

I've always been a fan of the Indian method. It relies

---

[10] Honda Motor Corporation, 1960s.

on being human and sorting things out for the greater good, rather than on the idle reassurance of so-called 'rules'. It's based on give 'n' take. Remove the oppressive tyranny of signage and controls, and the wit of humanity takes over. And it's better.

These different driving cultures don't mix very well, obviously. Put the Indian taxi driver in London or the Californian trucker in Bogota, and there will be a period of bafflement. So maybe the human condition isn't as universal as I first thought. But driving around in cars is a great way to reveal our differences, enjoy them, and maybe even heal some of them.

I like that.

Flying off on one

Once upon a time, the latest thing to have in your car was a gearstick on the inside, or a roof, or a radio. Now its aerodynamics and, especially, downforce.

Let's take a mythical new supercar, although it could in fact be one of many real ones. Let's say its makers boast that at 150mph, its aerodynamics produce 200kg of downforce. That means you can go round a corner on a track faster. But I see a problem with this, and now we're going to have to talk about aeroplanes, so I'm very excited.

The first thing to know is that pilots fly by something called the 'indicated airspeed', or IAS. It's displayed on a dial or screen on the instrument panel, and IAS is what governs how the aeroplane behaves. If it's about to stall, for example.

It's not the same as ground speed. Aeroplanes fly through the air as if the air is still, but in reality the body of air may be moving relative to the ground. So on a calm day the airspeed and the ground speed will be pretty much the same thing, but if you have a 20mph tailwind then an aeroplane flying at an indicated 100mph will be covering the ground at 120mph.

Turn around and fly the other way, and your 100mph aeroplane is doing 80mph across the land. That's all pretty obvious.

But there's something else, which is 'true airspeed' (bear with me a bit on this). Remember that the instruments 'know' the airspeed only by comparing the pressure of an oncoming stream of air down the 'pitot tube' with the pressure of static air. It's pretty crude, really. The instrument is calibrated to be accurate on something meteorologists call a Standard Atmospheric Day, which is a theoretical set of values for temperature, pressure and air density.

In reality, the atmosphere varies a lot. If you're flying at high altitude on a very hot day, the air is much thinner than this 'standard' atmosphere. Now when the airspeed indicator reads 100mph, the aeroplane might actually be doing 130mph. I'm trying to keep this unmathsy, but if you imagine that the molecules of air are more widely spaced, then the aeroplane must go faster to achieve the rate of airflow that equals our so-called 100mph.

Now back to the car. The speedo gives you ground speed, obviously. But let's imagine our racetrack is somewhere very high – La Paz in Bolivia, for example – and it's a hot day, and windy as well.

You approach that corner at 150mph, according to the speedo, but the air is thin and you have a tailwind. Your aerodynamic aids might be moving through the air at only 100mph. There goes a goodly chunk of your downforce. Oh dear.

Anyone have any thoughts on this?

Let's go vegan

Every time a piece of legislation comes along that we imagine threatens the car, the car actually improves.

Once, it was all about unleaded petrol. We'd get less power and more detonation, everyone said; but what we ended up with was engines with valves made from proper materials rather than the cheese from a school metalworking shop. Good.

Then it was catalytic converters. 'Strangling our engines!' cried car enthusiasts. Not so. The catalytic converter can be destroyed by unburnt fuel in the exhaust, so car makers were forced to use fuel injection and digital control on all cars, which led to higher specific outputs, better fuel economy, better reliability and more accurate trip computers. Without the cat, we'd all still be under the bonnet arsing about with carburettors.

It's not only legislation. Fashion and public opinion drive car makers (who are otherwise pretty lazy) to better things. Environmentalism has simply given us more efficient engines, which can't be a bad thing. The push for electric cars has improved battery technology, which is good for everyone.

So let's think about the growing calls for vegan car interiors. Morrissey (who once sang, 'Why pamper life's complexity/When the leather runs smooth on the passenger seeeeeeeeat') has asked GM to think about them. It's a good idea, and you don't need to be a vegan to think that.

Because if we don't ask, then the motor industry, which is deeply stuckist, will continue to slap leather over everything. This is how the thinking has gone for decades: poor people have seats covered in cloth left over at Vic Reeves's tailors and a plastic steering wheel; anyone vaguely posh has leather.

Meanwhile, look at all the amazing synthetic materials that have come along in the last twenty years, used for adventure clothing and the like. They're waterproof, breathable, wipe-downable, durable and available in any colour or pattern you can imagine. They're ideal for cars and would look cool. Why the hell do we want to drive around sitting on the remains of a cow? It's medieval at best.

Leather is a hopeless upholstery material and nothing more than a sociological hang-up. It's what the Romans used to make underpants.

Velour, on the other hand . . .

Volvo ruined my life

Some wealthy American business types stare from their office windows at a view of Central Park in Manhattan. Others, at the top of the Burj Khalifa in Dubai, can see the whole of the UAE. I know a man whose office is a wooden gazebo in his garden, and as he works he looks upon the merrie greenwood of olde England.

I look out of the window of my office on to the storage compound of a Volvo dealership.

One day, I'm going to have a Volvo estate. I've said this before, and I know it will happen. Not yet, because I'm not ready, and not tomorrow. Probably not for years, to be honest, but it will happen one day.

Sometimes I think the inevitability of eventual Volvo ownership means it's something I should simply get out of the way. Otherwise, it's a bit like pretending I don't need to go to the dentist.

But all that is for another time. It's not, in any case, why Volvo ruined my life. To understand that, we need to step back to *c.*1977.

I liked a girl called Susan (I've changed her name in case she's reading this. Her real name is Sally). Sue lived in a modern house, with a driveway along one side and a garage at the back. It was up this drive I would have to walk as a downy-faced new suitor to visit her than whom no fairer was.

Unfortunately, in walking up the drive I had to pass her dad's parked car, and it was a Volvo 244DL.

Younger readers should know that this car harked from a time when Volvos really weren't funky in any way whatsoever. The 244 had evolved from the earlier 140-series saloons, which had been designed by one of the directors' children using a ruler, a pencil and a coin to draw around for the wheels. It was a brutally functional car, from a time when the pragmatism and dourness of the Swedes made the Scots look like the Banana Splits.

The 240-series – available as a saloon, estate or two-door coupé (God knows how that happened) – developed the shape-of-a-Volvo philosophy quite radically, with a slightly sloping radiator grille. There must have been massive and heated meetings about this at Volvo board level, because it's difficult to see how it was necessary to introduce a rakish and unexpected angle other than 90 degrees to a modern Volvo. They had ruthlessly expunged the wanton curvaceousness of the P1800 and Amazon, and now this. Where would it end? With the V40. Bloody thing hasn't got a straight line on it anywhere.

Anyway. The sort of man who chose to drive a car as square as the 244 was not going to let me anywhere near his daughter. I knew that as soon as I rounded the corner and came face to face with its bluff front. It screamed 'Stop!' And I did.

I mean, he could have chosen a Rover SD1, Peugeot 504, Citroën GS, Ford Granada . . . any number of cars that were less boxy than the 244. Removal vans were less boxy than the 244, and they were designed to hold boxes. But no. He made a conscious choice to drive a car that said he didn't care for the frivolous or the unnecessary or even the faintly rounded off. The 244 was the least styled a car could be whilst still allowing the occupants to look out of windows.

So; Susan remained elusive, and I believe I was slightly retarded, sexually, by the Volvo 244. Who knows how different my life might have turned out if there'd been an Austin Princess on the drive. Even now, if I think about the Volvo 244, I feel the cold clutch of the unrequited on the trembling vestige of my teenage heart. Or something.

But do you know what really bothers me? Years later, when we had gone our separate ways, I learned that Susan's father had suddenly and unexpectedly run off with a much younger woman. In his Volvo.

Where's the justice in that?

Betta getta Jetta

Some men, when they reach their forties, buy a Harley-Davidson and a ridiculous tasselled jacket and then go on a tour of Europe or California's Highway One, leaving their wives and careers behind. This is the so-called mid-life crisis.

But what if it isn't available to you? What if you're a Premier League footballer or rock star, with a garage full of Lambos and Ducatis? It's not fair, unless we invent some sort of anti-crisis for people who want to turn their backs on the playboy lifestyle and seize the teenage dream of crashing normality.

I need to do more work on this, but the anti-crisis definitely requires some clear signposts for outside observers; the equivalent of that American V-twin in paragraph one, or a second-hand 911 and a leather jacket. Otherwise our former centre-forward could simply be mistaken for someone who'd always worked in financial management, rather than someone who'd made a life-changing decision. It needs to be obvious that, as the poet Larkin once put it, 'He chucked up everything and just cleared off.'

It must start with turning your back on the trappings of performance exotica and buying a truly boring car. The most boring car the world knows. And this begs a question: what is that car? It's the VW Jetta. Saloon.

I'm not saying the Jetta is a terrible car. I drove one once – with Jeremy Clarkson, in fact – and thought it was rather good. Tasteful, well made, undemanding. But wantonly workaday.

A genuinely bad car can be very interesting. I still recall with some fondness the absolute horror of the Citroën Pluriel. The Peugeot 2008 can stimulate with its potent fusion of mediocrity and mediocrity. Meanwhile, the Jetta is a car that does not dwell in your conscience in any way, rather like that long-handled spoon I have for retrieving pickled onions from the bottom of a jar. Bloody useful, that is, but I simply never think about it.[11]

I did a quick online search for a Jetta near me – used, obviously, because newness makes any car exciting. Within minutes I'd found the perfect example at Alan Day VW. Even the dealer doesn't really like it. The dash is photographed with the tank ¼ full, and the number plate appears to say 'shit'. Whoever specified this car was three years ahead of me and, I like to think, used to play for Manchester United.

It's the dark blue of an old bore's suit and comes on the standard wheels, with the default black cloth interior. It's the 1.4-litre petrol, not the more popular diesel, thus denying you an opportunity to 'interest' people with your views on low-range torque or the motorway cruise.

It's a car that genuinely says nothing about you, other than that you need a car. It's the car you'd end up with if they were available on the NHS. If you arrive at a point in your life where you crave an utterly ordinary car, you should have this one. It has no meaning.

---

[11] Though obviously I thought about it then.

Seriously, though: who would want a dark blue 1.4-litre petrol VW Jetta? Someone who doesn't give a pig's arse, and that's very cool. All credit to VW for being able to make a car that is in no way bad, but is so dazzlingly banal that it's as forgettable as a random Tuesday. It will be the last car to survive on Earth, parked somewhere in Dullsville, Arizona.

I'll take it.

Reviewed: walking

A bloke I know walks everywhere. I don't mean only to the shops and the pub; he lives and works in west London, but if he has to be at a meeting ten miles away, he will simply get up early and walk there, and back.

I suppose I should be grateful, because by not taking a car (he doesn't own one as far as I know) he is freeing up a bit of road space for my Rolls-Royce, which is generous. And I can't even repay him with a lift, because he'd rather walk.

Meanwhile, my own commute to the GT production office is just under two miles. I have discharged this by pretty much every means possible: cars, motorcycles, scooters, bicycles, the bus and the train. I haven't flown there yet, because the personal airship is not at the advanced state of development I expected by 2018, but it occurs to me that if I took a slightly circuitous route, I could even come by boat. But I never walk.

Walking: maybe there's something in it. Ironically enough, and after a fairly heavy weekend, I awoke this morning with a mouth like the bottom of one of Gandhi's sandals, and decided that a walk to work would sort me out.

Then I went a bit further and decided to give up fuel for a week. People give up booze for January and chocolate for Lent and that's all deeply unimaginative, but forgoing fuel for a random week in the spring is properly meaningless and irrelevant, so that's what I'm doing.

The No Fuel Rule does, of course, still allow me access to my 'collection of interesting bicycles'. Except it doesn't, because Richard Hammond is experimenting with cycling to work, which means the roads are host to a miniature roving ball of righteous Brummie fury, which makes the whole idea far too dangerous. Walking, then.

Out I stepped, suffused with mindfulness and well-being. There was lots to see. I stopped at a shop called 'Adventures in Furniture', because I'd had one once, many years ago, but nothing similar was on offer. So I moved on a few blocks and had a nice cappuccino whilst engaging with the community in the community. I loitered at a bookshop and moved a volume by Jeremy Clarkson into the medieval history section. I met a nice dog, bought some sweets and hid in a doorway when I saw someone doing a survey. It was a proper adventure.

After only twenty minutes I was staring wistfully through the window of the Honda motorcycle dealership next to our office, at a bike the exact copy of which was sitting silently in my garage. What were the benefits? In the long term, probably better pelvic articulation, stronger knees, superior deportment and improved chi energy flow.

But then a man drove past in a Porsche 911, and I realised that I'd gifted him a slightly improved drive as an act of pure and selfless philanthropy.

If that was you, you're welcome.

(In the next exciting instalment, our brave explorer

tries the same journey on the opposite side of the road, in case he missed anything interesting.)

Listen up you youngsters

For years, I've been listening to people telling me that the car will destroy the planet. And sometimes, their arguments have even been faintly convincing. But it turns out not to be a problem at all, because the car will die out from lack of interest before it does any permanent damage.

We were discussing on our car show the other day how the number of people taking the driving test in Britain has fallen by 70 per cent (?) in the last decade. We take this to mean young people, as older folk can either already drive or have decided, like my mate Ben (aged sixty), not to bother.

And as a result of this, new cars are becoming

boring, because they're just elaborate financial instruments designed to draw people into a lease scheme or hire-purchase deal, which is where the car industry is really making its money. No kid wants his dad to buy a Citroën Cactus in the way I was desperate for my dad to buy a Rover 3500, because they're more interested in Snapchat.

To be honest, if I were thirteen I would be more interested in Snapchat as well, but it hadn't been invented when I was a lad and one of the few things to get excited about in grimy and dysfunctional 1970s Britain was cars. So cars were what we dreamt about, when we'd finished thinking about Karen Bradley's emerging breasts.[12]

So it seems to make sense. The next generation isn't interested in cars, so cars are becoming dull.

But I've since thought about this a bit more, and it's a horse's arse. For a start, I'd forgotten that I was young once, but now I've recalled the experience I remember that a lot of cars were boring then as well. The Austin Allegro? The Morris Marina? The Hillman Hunter? I

---

[12] Her name has been changed in case she's actually reading this. Her real name was Deborah.

wouldn't wish these things on Donald Trump's barber, and I certainly didn't have posters of them on my wall. I had a Lamborghini Countach, and no one's dad could even begin to own one of those. And anyway, I've since driven one and that was crap as well.

No, the truth is that declining interest in cars is great news for those of us who still like them. Hold on a minute.

I'm forever hearing people on the radio and television lamenting how bell-ringing or morris dancing or wife-throwing are not drawing in the younger generation, and so they're going to die out. Everyone throws up their arms and goes, 'Oh no! There won't be any more (*insert dreary outmoded pastime*) once this generation has gone.'

So what? So long as some people from the current generation are interested in spoiling the experience of a pub garden by running around it with fairy bells on their boots, it will continue. The younger generation isn't in the least bit interested, so when it mercifully dies out, they won't care. So what's the problem? The dead are hardly going to be hacked off about it. They'll be too angry about being dead.

So it doesn't bother me in the slightest that my young nephews and nieces won't share my love of cars. I can continue with it as long as I'm alive, and, more to the point, they won't be cluttering up the road and spoiling it for me. When I'm gone, they can throw my Ferrari in the river and make a short and amusing video about it.

More to the point, this decline will improve cars. I've argued for decades that cars will eventually become a hobby, just as sailing boats and biplanes have. Nobody actually *needs* those things any more, so the ones that survive or are freshly made for enthusiasts are better than the ones we had when they were mere appliances and instruments of work.

The same will happen with cars. Once nobody needs a car simply as a means to move about (because we will have invented the antimatter air capsule) there won't be any dreary grey diesel hatchbacks available to drive away for £99 a month thevalueofyourcarmaygodownetcetc.

What car lover would want one of those? Car makers, if they want to remain players in the twilight of their business, will have to make affordable cars that are wonderful to drive. The roads will be populated by the likes of the MX-5 or a hot Clio.

Bring it on; I can't wait. Less traffic and better cars, all owned by people who are interested in what they're doing.

Thinking of learning to drive? Please don't.

Acknowledgements

I always hate this bit, where the author attempts to contrive some moving and sentimental tribute to the wife/husband and their forbearance and patience, plus the nod to the publisher's faith in the original idea, and how the cat/dog was an inspiration, drone drone drone.

Tell you what; I'd like to acknowledge the work of The Felix Project, a charity that redistributes surplus food to the needy. They could do with a few new vans. So I'm going to use the proceeds from this book to buy them one. That way, these random ramblings will at least have done some good, and columns about cars will have turned into a genuinely useful vehicle doing worthwhile work. I like that.

I should also thank Lucy Brown of DriveTribe for keeping the editorial side of things together. I'm sorry you wasted so much of your young life.

JAMES MAY

THE
REASSEMBLER

BBC FOUR

'A typically Mayesque celebration of classic engineering ... May
is extraordinarily good at explaining what a carburettor is or
outlining how a governor works... It's charming, transfixing
and surprisingly intimate...It might be the best thing he's ever
done.' – *Guardian* [review of BBC4 TV series]

'Reassembly is merely a form of therapy; something that stimulates a
part of my brain that is left wanting in my daily life. When I rebuild
a bicycle, I re-order my head. So might you...

I'm delighted that you will be holding in your hands a book about
putting things back together. It's a subject that fascinates me but which
I assumed was a lonely passion that I would take to the grave,
unconsummated by the normal channels of human interaction.

Welcome! You and I, we are not alone, and our screwdrivers are our
flashing Excaliburs as we sally forth to make small parts of the
fragmented world whole again.'

JAMES MAY

HOW TO LAND AN A330 AIRBUS

'James May is the best thing ever to come out of Top Gear'
-Radio Times

Being given yet another pointless 'man manual' that told him fifty ways to tie a bow tie in under 30 seconds made James May certain there was a need for another kind of book. This book, in fact.

He reckons there are nine vital things that a chap should be able to do. Not stuff you can download from the internet, but really important things. You never know when you might need to land an A330 Airbus, or deliver twins. And there may well be a moment when being able to play a bit of classical music on the piano is absolutely crucial to your success with women.

So read, learn and be prepared – you'll wonder how you ever lived without it.

Our world has been transformed beyond recognition, particularly in the twentieth century, and so were our lives and our aspirations.

Throughout *James May's Magnificent Machines*, our guide explores the iconic themes of the past hundred years: flight, space travel, television, mechanised war, medicine, computers, electronic music, skyscrapers, electronic espionage and much more.

But he also reveals the hidden story behind why some inventions like the Zeppelin, the hovercraft or the Theremin struggled to make their mark. He examines the tipping points – when technologies such as the car or the internet became unstoppable – and gets up close by looking at the nuts and bolts of remarkable inventions.

Packed with surprising statistics and intriguing facts, this is the ideal book for anyone who wants to know how stuff works and why some stuff didn't make it.

'James May is the best thing ever
to come out of Top Gear'
-Radio Times

**For at least two decades now modern man has been on the
brink of a crisis.**

Persuaded by both the post-feminist political landscape and his
representation in the popular media to remodel himself as an
endearingly hopeless halfwit, he now exists only as an object of pity.

James and his happy band of brothers (plus a few women, but we try to
edit them out) are engaged on a quest to lead maledom to a broad sunlit
upland strewn with slim books of English verse and neatly stacked with
correctly sharpened tools arranged in descending size order. From here
they confront the mysteries of romance and fashion, the cult of men's
cooking and the daunting underworld of hardcore DIY.

Read it and remember that, as a chap, your first duty is to be dependable.

And then you can have a pint.

**James May is back with his hilarious and controversial opinions
on . . . just about everything.**

As well as writing about his first love, cars, James has a go at political
correctness, the endless rules and regulations of daily life, the internal
combustion engine and traffic wardens. He discusses gastropubs,
Jeremy Clarkson and other trials of modern life.

His highly entertaining observations from behind the wheel will have
you laughing out loud, whether you share his opinions, or not.

Car Fever is an indispensable guide to life for the modern driver.